The Great Book of Riddles & Jokes

Published by :
Lotus Press Publishers & Distributors

Vivek Shukla

4735/22, Prakash Deep Building
Ansari Road, Darya Ganj,
New Delhi - 110002

Lotus Press : Publishers & Distributors
Unit No. 220, 2nd Floor, 4735/22, Prakash Deep Building,
Ansari Road, Darya Ganj, New Delhi- 110002
Ph.: 98118-38000
• E-mail : lotuspress1984@gmail.com
www.lotuspress.co.in

The Great Book of Riddles & Jokes

ISBN: 978-81-8382-261-9

Printed & Published by : **Lotus Press Publisher & Distributors,** New Delhi-02

PREFACE

Are you depressed or bored? Are you tired of the nine-to-five rat race and just having to deal with the mean-spirited people in the hateful, evil world? Then lighten up! Bring a little humour into your life. Humour enhances the soul, reduces depression, and makes life a little more enjoyable. We all need that!

Ever noticed how a person who is always serious is always boring? You will enjoy life more if you look for the humour in things.

Here are some examples of how you can add humour to your everyday life:

If someone asks me what are you up to, you may reply, "Six foot even."

If you're asked, "What's up?," You may reply, "The ceiling."

If someone asks you what's new, you can say, "New Delhi, New York, new shoes, new dress and pneumonia."

If you are driving down the road and are asked what did that last sign say, you may say, "Nothing, since signs don't have vocal cords."

There are many more examples like these.... Adding humour to your daily conversation will get a lot of eye rolls and chuckles too.

Read this book the first time just for laughs. You'll get plenty.

Then read it again to develop a more humorous mind-set.

This book is designed to bring some happiness into the world. Ever wish you could find the world's best jokes and riddles collected into one place? These jokes and riddles are to the point with no excess verbiage. They are neatly divided into two sections— jokes and riddles.

We all have heard jokes and riddles like these a million times. We've pestered our families and friends with them. Why? They crack us up! Nothing feels better than a good laugh. The book ranges widely and becomes in a sense a discussion of comedy, at least in this limited area, and of its social and psychological implications. The work is freely illustrated with all manner of pictures and folly drawn from widely varied sources.

A collection of the world's best humour, besides having readers double up with laughter, this book will also set them thinking, as these jokes and humorous anecdotes contain significant moral and ethical insights.

This book will also motivate you to think positively, inspire you by stirring the creative juices, stimulate the genius in you, develop your moral values, help flower your personality and improve your sense of humour, while simultaneously providing practical wisdom from all over the world.

The book is just the kind of humour that men and women across all age-groups would enjoy immensely and learn from.

Author

CONTENTS

Part I: Riddles

PART I RIDDLES

CHAPTER 1

Basic Riddles

Climbing Snail

A snail is at the bottom of a 20 metres deep pit. Every day the snail climbs 5 metres upwards, but at night it slides 4 metres back downwards.

How many days does it take before the snail reaches the top of the pit?

Solution

On the first day, the snail reaches a height of 5 metres and slides down 4 metres at night, and thus ends at a height of 1 metre.

On the second day, he reaches 6 metres, but slides back to 2 metres.

On the third day, he reaches 7 metres, but slides back to 3 metres.

On the fifteenth day, he reaches 19 metres, but slides back to 15 metres.

On the sixteenth day, he reaches 20 metres, so now he is at the top of the pit!

Conclusion: The snail reaches the top of the pit on the 16th day!

Segmented Numbers

Of all the numbers whose literal representations in capital letters consists only of straight line segments (for example, FIVE), only one number has a value equal to the number of segments used to write it.

Which number has this property?

Solution

This is the only solution that satisfies the requirement that the capital letters shall consist only of straight line segments:

TWENTY-NINE

Ram and Shyam

Ram is standing behind Shyam and at the same time Shyam is standing behind Ram.

How is this possible?

Solution

Ram and Shyam are standing with their backs towards each other!

Tall Boys

Rohit is taller than Dhruv, Jatin is shorter than Rohit.

Only one of the following statements is correct:

1. Dhruv is taller than Jatin.
2. Jatin is taller than Dhruv.
3. It cannot be determined if Jatin or Dhruv is tallest.

Which of the statements is correct?

Solution

Statement 3 is correct. The only thing that can be stated for sure is that Rohit is tallest.

Abracadabra with Apples

In Miss Miranda's class are eleven children. Miss Miranda has a bowl with eleven apples. Miss Miranda wants to divide the eleven apples among the children of her class, in such a way that each child in the end has an apple, but one apple still remains in the bowl.

Can you help Miss Miranda?

Solution

Ten children get a single apple, and the eleventh gets the bowl with an apple still in it.

Tour de France

In the Tour de France, what is the position of a rider, after he passes the second placed rider?

Solution

Second!

Chain Connection

You have five pieces of chain, each consisting of three links. You want to make one long chain of these five pieces. Breaking open a link costs 1 Re, and welding an open link costs 3 Rs.

Is it possible to make one long chain of the five pieces, if you have just 15 Rs?

Solution

Yes, this is possible. First, break open all three links of one of the pieces of chain. This costs $3 \times 1 = 3$ Rs. Then join the remaining four pieces of chain with the three open links. Welding these links costs $3 \times 3 = 9$ Rs. The total costs are 12 Rs.

Poor and Rich

The poor have it,

the rich want it,

but if you eat it you will die.

What is this?

Solution

Nothing!

Twins Trouble

Jatin and Varun are brothers. "We are born within the same hour," says Jatin, "On the same day of the same year."

"But," says Varun, "we are no twins!"

How is this possible?

Solution

Jatin and Varun are part of a set of triplets, or quadruplets, or even more.

Interesting Note: The situation that Jatin and Varun would have the same father but not the same mother, is not a valid solution, because Jatin and Varun would then be half-brothers!

One, Two, Three

Using the digits 1 up to 9, three numbers (of three digits each) can be formed, such that the second number is twice the first number, and the third number is three times the first number.

Which are these three numbers?

Solution

There are four solutions:

192, 384, and 576.

219, 438, and 657.

273, 546, and 819.

327, 654, and 981.

Ten Trees

Joyce has bought ten trees for her garden. She wants to plant these trees in five rows, with four trees in each row.

First Question: How must Joyce plant the trees?

Another Question: Joyce's neighbour Gagan has bought nine trees for his garden. How can he plant these nine trees in ten rows, with three trees in each row?

Solution 1

The trees must be planted on the edges of a five pointed star:

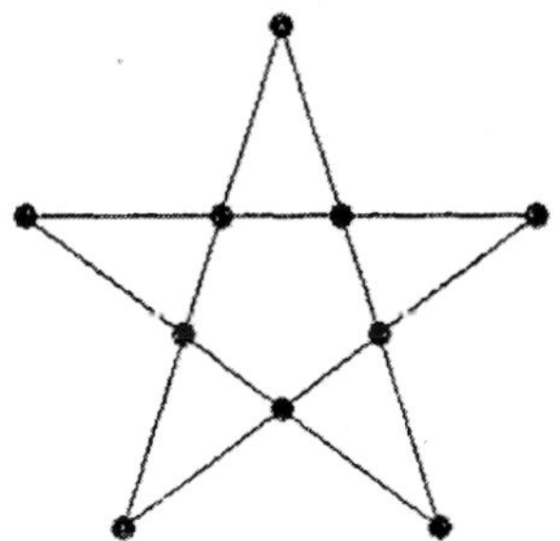

Solution 2

The nine trees must be planted as follows:

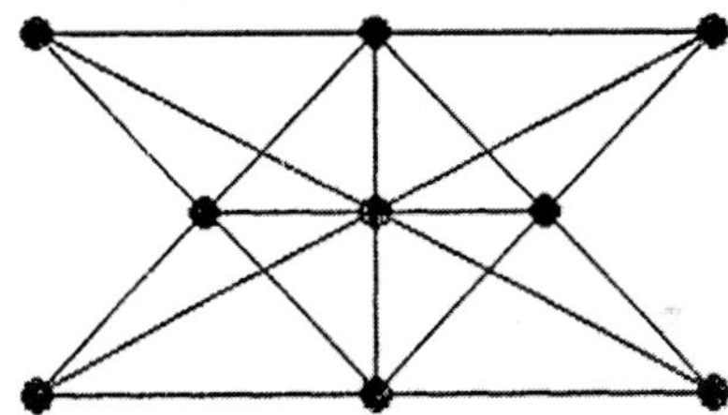

Consecutive Elements

The objects in this row have something in common:

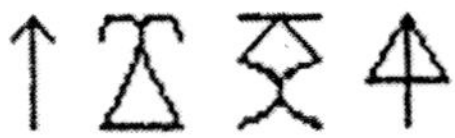

One of the following three objects is the next element in the row.

Which one is the next element?

Solution to

If you look closely to the objects, you will see that the first one is the number 1 concatenated with its mirror image. The second object consists of number 2 and its mirror image, and so on...

Conclusion: The next element of ↑ is !...

Birthday Cake

The birthday cake shown here must be cut into eight equally sized pieces. However, you are allowed to make only 3 straight cuts.

How can the cake be cut into eight pieces with only 3 straight cuts?

Solution to

There is only one solution which solves the problem with three straight cuts, and leaves exactly eight equally shaped portions. One should cut the cake two times vertically in a '+' shape across the top and make the third cut horizontally in the middle of the cake (looking at the cake from the front), as shown in the figure. The disadvantage of this solution is however that only four portions will contain fruit-decoration etc., whereas the other four portions will only contain bottom parts of the cake...

This is how the cake could be cut (seen from above), if we would prefer to have both top and bottom parts in each piece:

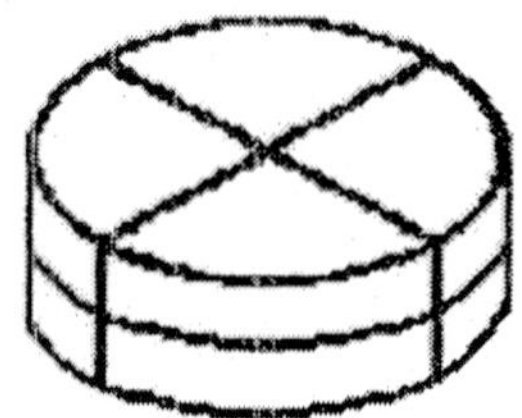

Finally, a solution that requires some rearrangement of the pieces after the first two cuts, is the following: like before, make the first two cuts cross-wise, then arrange all four pieces in a row, and make the third straight cut like this:

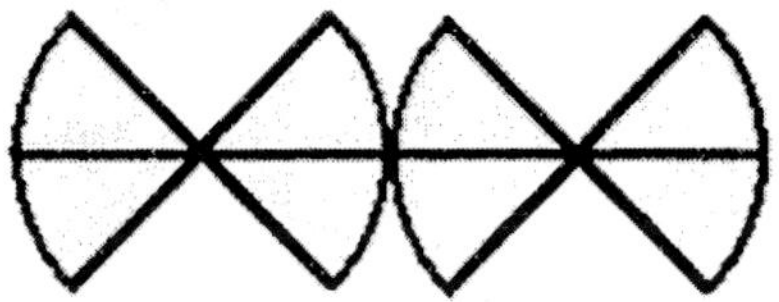

Silly Statements

Below are a number of statements:

Precisely one of these statements is untrue.

Precisely two of these statements are untrue.

Precisely three of these statements are untrue.

Precisely four of these statements are untrue.

Precisely five of these statements are untrue.

Precisely six of these statements are untrue.

Precisely seven of these statements are untrue.

Precisely eight of these statements are untrue.

Precisely nine of these statements are untrue.

Precisely ten of these statements are untrue.

Which of these statements is true?

Solution

The ten statements all contradict each other. So there can be at most one statement true. Now suppose there is no statement true. That would mean that statement 10 indeed would be true, which results in a contradiction. This means that exactly nine statements must be untrue, and thus only statement 9 is true.

Easy Equation

Each of the digits 1 up to 6 must be used exactly once in a multiplication of the following form:

... × ... = ...

How should the six digits be placed?

Solution

$3 \times 54 = 162$

Happy Birthday

When Sunita had her birthday in the year 2000 she became 8 years old. But she was born in the year 2008.

How can you explain this?

Solution

Sunita was born in 2008 BC.

Splitting Shapes

The shape shown below must be partitioned into four identical pieces (pieces may be upside down).

There are two ways in which this can be done. Which are these two ways?

Solution

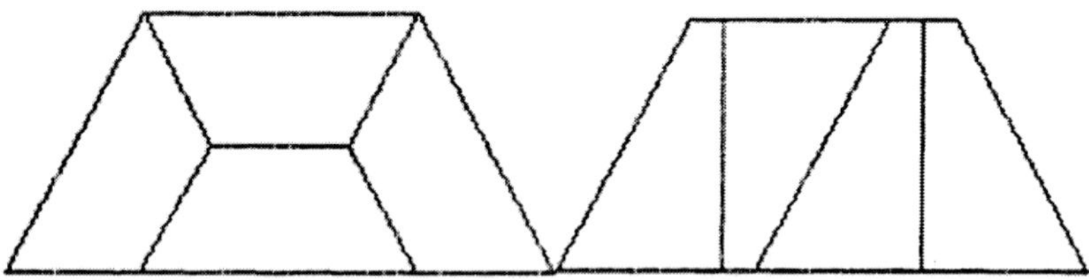

Another Question

The shape shown below must be partitioned into four identical pieces (pieces may be upside down).

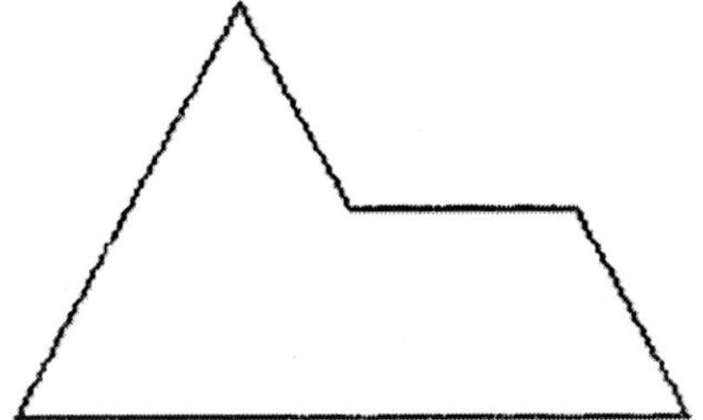

There are two ways in which this can be done. Which are these two ways?

Solution

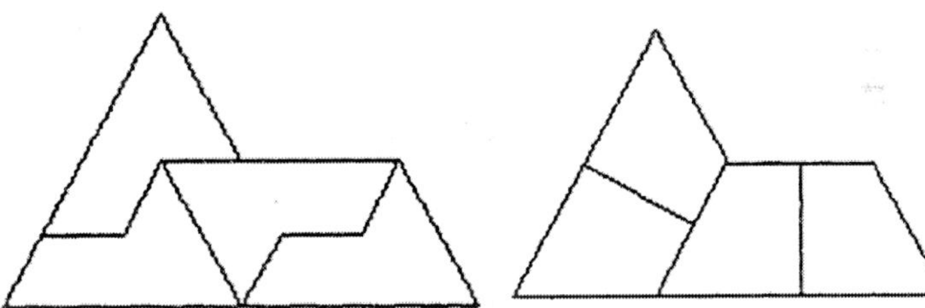

Another Question

The shape shown below must be partitioned into three identical pieces.

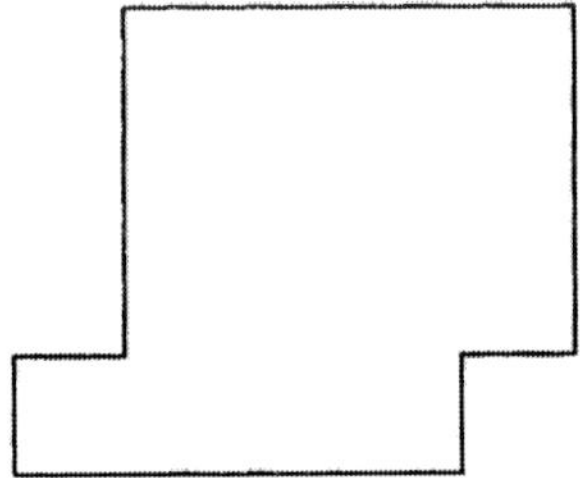

How can this be done?

Solution

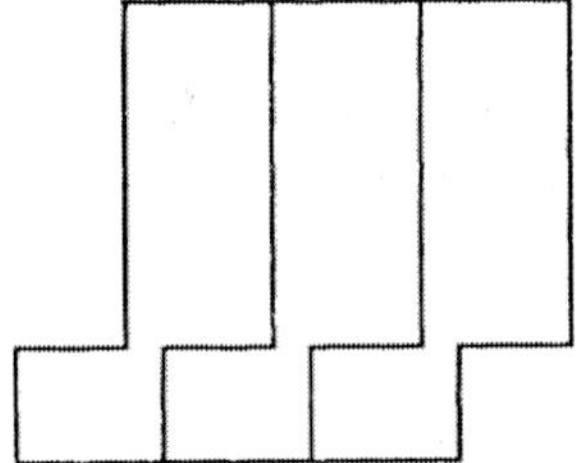

Smaller Squares

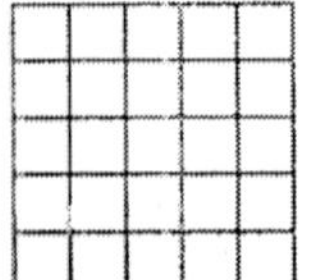

You can see a square of 5 by 5 smaller squares. The purpose is to divide the square along the lines in four pieces, in such a way that you can make two smaller squares with these four pieces, without needing to rotate the pieces.

How should this be done?

Solution

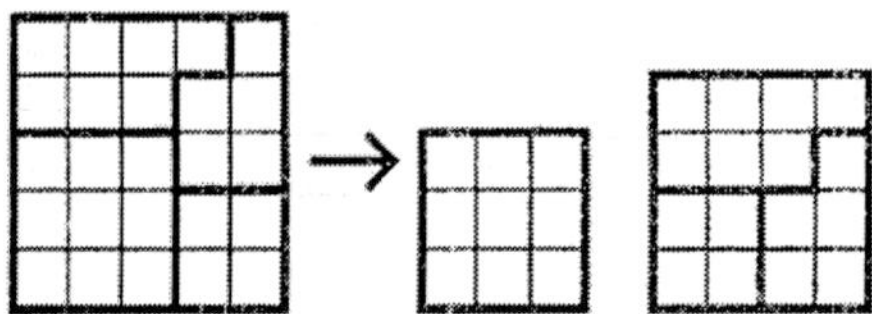

Plus Puzzle

The six puzzle pieces shown here can be combined into a symmetrical plus sign.

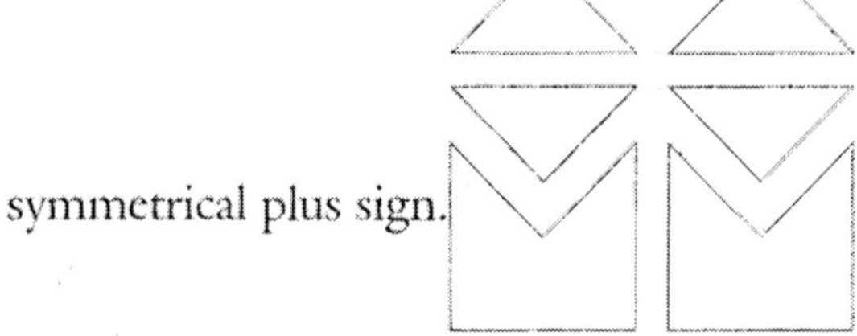

How can this be done?

Solution

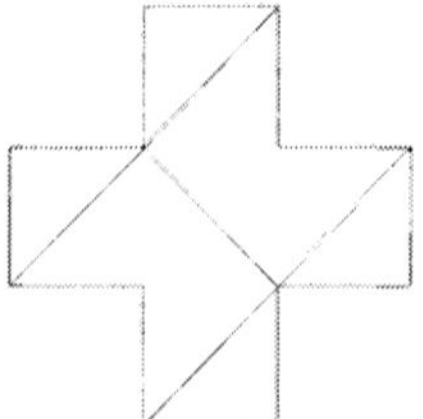

■■■

Chapter 2

Logical Puzzles

Old Masters

Three friends Pankaj, Dhruv and Henri are talking to each other about the art collection of Leonardo. Pankaj says: "Leonardo has at least four paintings of Rembrandt." Dhruv says: "No, he has less than four paintings of Rembrandt." "According to me," says Henri, "Leonardo has at least one Rembrandt."

If you known that only one of the three friends is right, how many Rembrandts does Leonardo possess?

Solution

Take a look at the statements about the number of paintings of Rembrandt. If Pankaj would be right ("at least four"), then Henri ("at least one") would also be right. If Henri would be right ("at least one"), then or Pankaj ("at least four") or Dhruv ("less than four") would also be right. So this means only Dhruv can be right and Leonardo possesses less than one Rembrandt, so no Rembrandt at all.

The Wolf, the Goat, and the Cabbage

A man has a wolf, a goat, and a cabbage. He must cross a river with the two animals and the cabbage. There is a small rowing-boat, in which he can take only one thing with him at a time. If, however, the wolf and the goat are left alone, the wolf will eat the goat. If the goat and the cabbage are left alone, the goat will eat the cabbage.

How can the man get across the river with the two animals and the cabbage?

Solution

There are two solutions:

First, the man takes the goat across, leaving the wolf with the cabbage. Then he goes back. Next, he takes the wolf across. Then the man goes back, taking the goat with him. After this, he takes the cabbage across. Then he goes back again, leaving the wolf with the cabbage. Finally, he takes the goat across.

First, the man takes the goat across, leaving the wolf with the cabbage. Then he goes back. Next, he takes the cabbage across. Then the man goes back, taking the goat with him. After this, he takes the wolf across. Then he goes back again, leaving the wolf with the cabbage. Finally, he takes the goat across.

Sock Search

In your bedroom you have a drawer with 2 red, 4 yellow, 6 purple, 8 brown, 10 white, 12 green, 14 black, 16 blue, 18 grey, and 20 orange socks. It is dark in your bedroom, so you can't distinguish between the colours of the socks.

How many socks do you need to take out of the drawer to be sure that you have at least three pairs of socks of the same colour?

Solution

In the worst case in which you didn't take three pairs of socks of the same colour, you took 2 red socks, 4 yellow socks, and 5 of each of the other colours. That's a total of 46 socks. Then if you take one more sock, you are sure to have 6 socks of at least one colour. So you have to take 47 socks from the drawer to be sure that you have at least three pairs of socks of the same colour.

Absurd Answers

Here are three answers:

Answer A

Answer A or B

Answer B or C

There is only one correct **Answer** to this question. Which **Answer** is this?

Solution

If **Answer** A would be correct, then **Answer** B ("**Answer** A or B") would also be correct. If **Answer** B would be correct, then **Answer** C ("**Answer** B or C") would also be correct. This leads to the conclusion that if either **Answer** A or **Answer** B would be the correct answer, there are at least two correct answers. This contradicts with the statement that "there is only one correct **Answer** to this question". If **Answer** C would be correct, then there are no contradictions.

So the solution is: **Answer** C.

Growing Water-Lily

In the middle of a round pool lies a beautiful water-lily. The water-lily doubles in size every day. After exactly 20 days the complete pool will be covered by the lily.

After how many days will half of the pool be covered by the water-lily?

Solution

Because the water-lily doubles its size every day and the complete pool is covered after 20 days, half of the pool will be covered one day before that, after 19 days.

Conclusion: After 19 days half of the pool will be covered by the water-lily

Jolly Jugs

You are standing next to a well, and you have two jugs. One jug has a content of 3 litres and the other one has a content of 5 litres. How can you get just 4 litres of water using only these two jugs?

Solution

Solution 1

Fill the 5 litre jug. Then fill the 3 litre jug to the top with water from the 5 litre jug. Now you have 2 litres of water in the 5 litre jug. Dump out the 3 litre jug and pour what's in the 5 litre jug into the 3 litre jug. Then refill the 5 litre jug, and fill up the 3 litre jug to the top. Since there were already 2 litres of water in the 3 litre jug, 1 litre is removed from the 5 litre jug, leaving 4 litres of water in the 5 litre jug.

Solution 2

Fill the 3 litre jug and pour it into the 5 litre jug. Then refill the 3 litre jug and fill up the 5 litre jug to the top. Since there were already 3 litres of water in the 5 litre jug, 2 litres of water are removed from the 3 litre jug, leaving 1 litre of water in the 3 litre jug. Then dump out the 5 litre jug and pour what's in the 3 litre jug into the 5 litre jug. Refill the 3 litre jug and pour it into the 5 litre jug. Now you have 4 litres of water in the 5 litre jug.

Turning Cards

The following four cards sit on a table:

Each card has a digit on one side and a letter on the other side.

Which cards should you turn around to test the following statement: "when there is a vowel on one side of a card, then there is an even digit on the other side"?

Solution

You should turn the cards with the "E" and the "7".

The "E" should be turned to verify that there is an even digit on the other side. When there is an odd digit on the other side, the statement is not true.

The "7" should be turned to verify that there is no vowel on the other side. When there is a vowel on the other side, the statement is not true.

The "V" does not need to be turned; it is not a vowel and therefore it doesn't matter what kind of digit is on the other side.

The "2" also doesn't need to be turned. Whether there is a vowel or a consonant on the other side, the card always satisfies the statement: after all, it is not stated that only cards with a vowel have an even digit on the other side

Guess What

Madhu has one of the numbers 1, 2, or 3 in mind. Sophie is allowed to ask one question to Madhu to find out which of these three numbers he has in mind. Madhu will **Answer** this question only with the answers "yes", "no", or "I don't know".

Which question should Sophie ask Madhu to find out in one time which number he has in mind?

Solution

Sophie could for example ask Madhu the following: "I have the number 1 or 2 in mind. Is the number that you have in mind larger than the number I have in mind?" The **Answer** "yes" means that Madhu has the number 3 in mind, "I don't know" means 2, and "no" means 1.

Tick-Tack-Toe

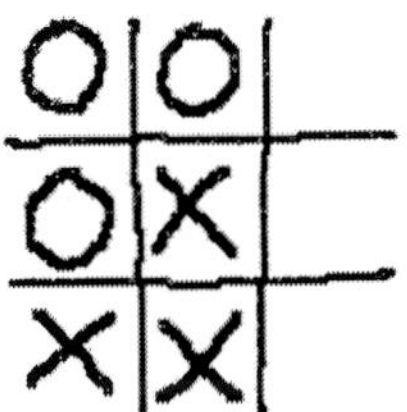

Vaid and Anjali play a game of tick-tack-toe. In this game, the

players try to get three circles or three crosses in a row (horizontal, vertical, or diagonal).

They follow the following rules:

A player always tries to win: if a player can place his own symbol (X or O) in a row which already contains two of his own symbols, he will do so.

A player always tries to avoid that his opponent wins: if a player can place his own symbol (X or O) in a row which already contains two of the symbols of his opponent, he will do so.

Of course, the first rule has precedence over the second rule, because the game can be won in this way.

In the game shown on the right, 6 moves have been done. Vaid plays with crosses (X) and Anjali plays with circles (0). However, we don't know who started the game.

Who will win this game?

Solution

It is clear that if we know who made the sixth move, we also know who can make the seventh move and wins.

If Anjali (circles) has made the sixth move, there are three possibilities for the situation after five moves:

Possibility 1:

o		
o	x	
x	x	

Possibility 2:

	o	
o	x	
x	x	

Possibility 3:

o	o	
	x	
x	x	

Based on the rules of the game only possibility 1 could have resulted in the situation after six moves. In that case, there are three possibilities for the situation after four moves:

Possibility 1:

o		
o	x	
	x	

Possibility 2:

o		
o		
x	x	

Possibility 3:

o		
o	x	
x		

Based on the rules of the game, Vaid (crosses) would have made the winning move, which however didn't happen. From this, we can conclude that Vaid did not make the fifth move and Anjali did not make the sixth move. So, it must have been Vaid who made the sixth move and Anjali can make the seventh, winning move!

To check that Vaid could indeed have made the sixth move, we look at the the following three possibilities after five moves:

Possibility 1:

O	O	
O		
X	X	

Possibility 2:

O	O	
O	X	
X		

Possibility 3:

O	O	
O	X	
	X	

Based on the rules of the game, only possibility 3 can result in the situation after six moves. So, Vaid could indeed have made the sixth move.

The Round Table

Yesterday evening, Ritu and her husband invited their neighbours (two couples) for a dinner at home. The six of them sat at a round table. Ritu tells you the following:

"Vicky sat on the left of the woman who sat on the left of the man who sat on the left of Anna.

Eshant sat on the left of the man who sat on the left of the woman who sat on the left of the man who sat on the left of the woman who sat on the left of my husband.

Jimmy sat on the left of the woman who sat on the left of Rohit.

I did not sit beside my husband."

The Question: What is the name of Ritu's husband?

Solution

From the second statement, we know that the six people sat at the table in the following way (clockwise and starting with Ritu's husband):

Ritu's husband, woman, man, woman, man, Eshant

Because Ritu did not sit beside her husband, the situation must be as follows:

Ritu's husband, woman, man, Ritu, man, Eshant

The remaining woman must be Anna, and combining this with the first statement, we arrive at the following situation:

Ritu's husband, Anna, man, Ritu, Vicky, Eshant

Because of the third statement, Jimmy and Rohit can be placed in only one way, and we now know the complete order:

Ritu's husband Rohit, Anna, Jimmy, Ritu, Vicky, Eshant

Conclusion: the name of Ritu's husband is Rohit.

Happy Handshaking

Arun and his wife went to a party where four other married couples were present. Every person shook hands with everyone he or she was not acquainted with. When the handshaking was over, Arun asked everyone, including his own wife, how many hands they shook. To his surprise, Arun got nine different answers.

How many hands did Arun's wife shake?

Solution

Because, obviously, no person shook hands with himself or herself, or with his or her partner, nobody shook hands with more than eight other people. And since nine people shook hands with different numbers of people, these numbers must be 0, 1, 2, 3, 4, 5, 6, 7, and 8.

The person who shook 8 hands, shook hands with all other persons (who therefore shook each at least 1 hand), except with his or her partner. Therefore, the partner of the person who shook 8 hands, must be the person who shook 0 hands.

The person who shook 7 hands, shook hands with all other persons (who therefore shook each at least 2 hands), except with his or her partner and the person who shook 0 hands. Therefore, the partner of the person who shook 7 hands, must be the person who shook 1 hand.

The person who shook 6 hands, shook hands with all other persons (who therefore shook each at least 3 hands), except with his or her partner and the persons who shook 1 and 0 hands. Therefore, the partner of the person who shook 6 hands, must be the person who shook 2 hands.

The person who shook 5 hands, shook hands with all other persons (who therefore shook each at least 4 hands), except with his or her partner and the persons who shook 2, 1, and 0 hands. Therefore, the partner of the person who shook 5 hands, must be the person who shook 3 hands.

The only person left, is the one who shook 4 hands, and which must be Arun's wife. The **Answer** is: Arun's wife shook 4 hands.

Lighting Bulb

A light bulb is hanging in a room. Outside of the room there are three switches, of which only one is connected to the lamp. In the starting situation, all switches are 'off' and the bulb is not lit.

If it is allowed to check in the room only once to see if the bulb is lit or not (this is not visible from the outside), how can you determine with which of the three switches the light bulb can be switched on?

Solution

To find the correct switch (1, 2, or 3), turn switch 1 to 'on' and leave it like that for a few minutes. After that you turn switch 1 back to 'off', and turn switch 2 to 'on'. Now enter the room. If the light bulb is lit, then you know that switch 2 is connected to it. If the bulb is not lit, then it has to be switch 1 or 3. Now touching for short the light bulb, will give you the **Answer:** if the bulb is still hot, then switch 1 was the correct one; if the bulb is cold, then it has to be switch 3.

Apples and Pears

Tarun has three boxes with fruits in his barn: one box with apples, one box with pears, and one box with both apples and pears. The boxes have labels that describe the contents, but none of these labels is on the right box.

How can Tarun, by taking only one piece of fruit from one box, determine what each of the boxes contains?

Solution

Tarun takes a piece of fruit from the box with the labels 'Apples and Pears'. If it is an apple, then the label 'Apples' belong to this box. The box that said 'Apples', then of course shouldn't be labeled 'Apples and Pears', because that would mean that the box with 'Pears' would have been labeled correctly, and this is contradictory to the fact that none of the labels was correct. On the box with the label 'Apples' should be the label 'Pears'. If Tarun would have taken a pear, the reasoning would have been in a similar way.

Fun with Fuses...

Assume that you have a number of long fuses, of which you only know that they burn for exactly one hour after you lighted them at one end. However, you don't know whether they burn with constant speed, so the first half of the fuse can be burnt in only ten minutes while the rest takes the other fifty minutes to burn completely. Also assume that you have a lighter.

How can you measure exactly three quarters of an hour with these fuses?

Solution

With only two fuses that burn exactly one hour, one can measure three quarters of an hour accurately, by lighting the first fuse at both ends and the other fuse at one end simultaneously. When the first fuse is burnt out after exactly half an hour (!) you know that the second fuse still has exactly half an hour to go before it will be burnt completely, but we won't wait for that. We will now also light the other end of the second fuse. This means that the second fuse will now be burnt completely after another quarter of an hour, which adds up to exactly three quarters of an hour since we started lighting the first fuse!

Chess-board Chunks

Carefully see the chess-board. We want to cut the chess-board paper into pieces (over the lines!) such that each piece has twice as much squares of one colour than of the other colour (i.e. twice as much black squares as white squares or twice as much white squares as black squares).

Is this possible? Give a proof!

Solution

No, it is not possible to cut the chess-board paper into pieces such that each piece has twice as much squares of one colour than of the other colour.

If it would be possible, then every piece would have a number of squares divisible by 3 (because if a piece has n squares of one colour and $2 \times n$ squares of the other colour, it has $3 \times n$ squares in total). The total number of squares of all pieces would then also be divisible by 3. This is, however, impossible since the total number of squares on the chess-board is 64, which is not divisible by 3.

Little Lies

Raghu is a strange liar. He lies on six days of the week, but on the seventh day he always tells the truth. He made the following statements on three successive days:

Day 1: "I lie on Monday and Tuesday."

Day 2: "Today, it's Thursday, Saturday, or Sunday."

Day 3: "I lie on Wednesday and Friday."

The Question: On which day does Raghu tell the truth?

Solution

We know that Raghu tells the truth on only a single day of the week. If the statement on day 1 is untrue, this means that he tells the truth on Monday or Tuesday. If the statement on day 3 is untrue, this means that he tells the truth on Wednesday or Friday. Since Raghu tells the truth on only one day, these statements cannot both be untrue. So, exactly one of these statements must be true, and the statement on day 2 must be untrue.

Assume that the statement on day 1 is true. Then the statement on day 3 must be untrue, from which follows that Raghu tells the truth on Wednesday or Friday. So, day 1 is a Wednesday or a Friday. Therefore, day 2 is a Thursday or a Saturday. However, this would imply that the statement on day 2 is true, which is impossible. From this we can conclude that the statement on day 1 must be untrue.

This means that Raghu told the truth on day 3 and that this day is a Monday or a Tuesday. So day 2 is a Sunday or a Monday. Because the statement on day 2 must be untrue, we can conclude that day 2 is a Monday.

So day 3 is a Tuesday. Therefore, the day on which Raghu tells the truth is Tuesday.

Square Circles

Given are the following three equations:

■● = ▲

■ = ●◆

▲▲ = ◆◆◆

How many circles is a square, if you take the ratios in the three given equations; in other words: how many circles should be on the dots below? ■ =

Solution

= { according to equation 2 }

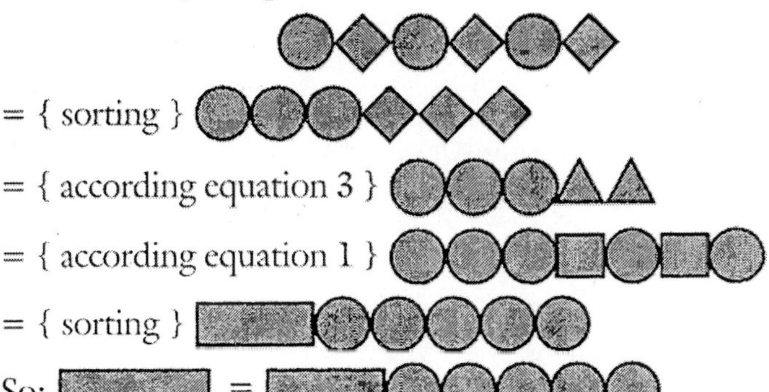

= { sorting }

= { according equation 3 }

= { according equation 1 }

= { sorting }

So: =

from which follows that =

Therefore the **Answer** is: 5 circles.

Placing Bricks

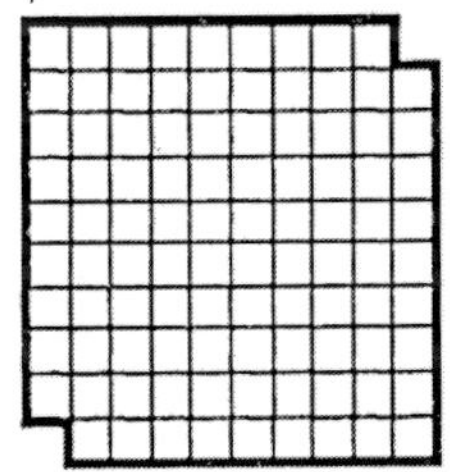

Try to fill the total board (10 × 10-2) with bricks of size 2 (and), so no overlaps, no gaps, and no bricks crossing the borders. Is this possible? (Proof!)

Solution

Imagine the board to be coloured like a chess-board. Each brick will cover a white and a black square of the board, so the number of bricks equals the number of white squares equals the number of black squares. But by removing the two opposite corners of the chess-board (with an even numbers of rows and columns), two squares of the same colour are removed, so there is an imbalance of white and black squares.

Conclusion: No, you can not fill the board.

Another Question

How many squares are present in the picture of the board?

Solution

Here is an overview of the number of squares of each size, as they are present in the figure:

9×9: 22 - 2 = 2

8×8: 32 - 2 = 7

7×7: 42 - 2 = 14

6×6: 52 - 2 = 23

5×5: 62 - 2 = 34

4×4: 72 - 2 = 47

3×3: 82 - 2 = 62

2×2: 92 - 2 = 79

1×1: 102 - 2 = 98

———————— +

Total: 366 squares.

Troubled Traveller

A traveller, on his way to Calicut, reaches a road junction, where he can turn left or right. He knows that only one of the two roads leads to Calicut, but unfortunately, he does not know which one. Fortunately, he sees two twin-brothers standing at the road junction, and he decides to ask them for directions.

The traveller knows that one of the two brothers always tells the truth and the other one always lies. Unfortunately, he does not know which one always tells the truth and which one always lies.

How can the traveller find out the way to Calicut by asking just one question to one of the two brothers?

Solution

The question that the traveller should ask is: "Does the left road lead to Calicut according to your brother?" If the **Answer** is "Yes", the traveller should turn right, and if the **Answer** is "No", the traveller should turn left.

Explanation: There are four possible cases:

The traveller asks the question to the truth-telling brother, and the left road leads to Calicut. The truth-telling brother knows that his lying brother would say that the left road does not lead to Calicut, and so he answers "No".

The traveller asks the question to the truth-telling brother, and the right road leads to Calicut. The truth-telling brother knows that his lying brother would say that the left road leads to Calicut, and so he answers "Yes".

The traveller asks the question to the lying brother, and the left road leads to Calicut. The lying brother knows that his truth-telling brother would say that the left road leads to Calicut, and so he lies "No".

The traveller asks the question to the lying brother, and the right road leads to Calicut. The lying brother knows that his truth-telling brother would say that the left road does not lead to Calicut, and so he lies "Yes".

At School

The gentlemen Dutch, English, Painter, and Writer are all teachers at the same secondary school. Each teacher teaches two different subjects. Furthermore:

Three teachers teach Dutch language

There is only one math teacher

There are two teachers for chemistry

Two teachers, Shankar and Mister English, teach history

Pankaj doesn't teach Dutch language

Sanjay is chemistry teacher

Mister Dutch doesn't teach any course that is taught by Karan or Mister Painter.

What is the full name of each teacher and which two subjects does each one teach?

Solution to

Since Pankaj as only one doesn't teach Dutch language, and Mister Dutch doesn't teach any course that is taught by Karan or Mister Painter, it follows that Pankaj and Mister Dutch are the same person and that he is at least math teacher. Shankar and Mister English both teach history, and are also among the three Dutch teachers. Pankaj Dutch therefore has to teach next to math, also chemistry. Because Sanjay is also chemistry teacher, he cannot be Mister English or Mister Painter, so he must be Mister Writer. Since Karan and Mister Painter are two different persons, just like Shankar and Mister English, the names of the other two teachers are Karan English and Shankar Painter.

Summarized:

Pankaj Dutch, math and chemistry

Sanjay Writer, Dutch and chemistry

Shankar Painter, Dutch and history

Karan English, Dutch and history.

Chapter 3

Math Riddles

Big Numbers

Using the digits 1 up to 9, two numbers must be made. The product of these two numbers should be as large as possible. All digits must be used exactly once.

Which are the requested two numbers?

Solution to

The digits of the requested two numbers obviously form descending sequences. Furthermore, if you have two pairs of numbers with equal sums, the pair of which the numbers have the smallest absolute difference, is the one of which the numbers have the largest product. Using this knowledge, the two numbers can easily be constructed by placing the digits one by one, starting with 9 and ending with 1:

9		96		964		9642		9642
	->		->		->		->	
8		87		875		8753		87531

The requested two numbers are 9642 and 87531.

Boys and Girls

Rahul and Priya have two children. The probability that the first child is a girl, is 50%. The probability that the second child is a girl, is also 50%. Rahul and Priya tell you that they have a daughter.

What is the probability that their other child is also a girl?

Solution to

There are four possibilities for two children:

	First child:	Second child:
1	girl	girl
2	girl	boy
3	boy	girl
4	boy	boy

The fourth possibility drops out, because Rahul and Priya have a daughter (so either the first or the second child is a girl). Therefore, three possibilities remain, of which in one case the other child is also a girl. So, the probability is 1/3 (about 33%).

Train Trouble

Arjun walks over a railway-bridge. At the moment that he is just ten metres away from the middle of the bridge, he hears a train coming from behind. At that moment, the train, which travels at a speed of 90 km/h, is exactly as far away from the bridge as the bridge measures in length. Without hesitation, Arjun rushes straight towards the train to get off the bridge. In this way, he misses the train by just four metres! If Arjun would, however, have rushed exactly as fast in the other direction, the train would have hit him eight metres before the end of the bridge.

What is the length of the railway-bridge?

Solution

Let the length of the bridge be x metres.

Running towards the train, Arjun covers $0.5\,x$-10 metres in the time that the train travels x-4 metres. Running away from the train, Arjun covers $0.5x+2$ metres in the time that the train travels $2x$-8 metres.

Because their speeds are constant, the following holds:

$(0.5x-10) / (x-4) = (0.5x+2) / (2x-8)$

which can be rewritten to

$0.5x^2 - 24x + 88 = 0$

Using the *abc* formula we find that $x=44$, so the railway-bridge has a length of 44 metres.

Ankit's Chickens

Farmer Ankit has a chicken farm. On a certain day, Ankit calculates in how many days he will run out of chicken-food. He notices that if he would sell 75 of his chickens, he could feed the remaining chickens twenty days longer with the chicken-food he has, and that if he would buy 100 extra chickens, he would run out of chicken-food fifteen days earlier.

How many chickens does farmer Ankit have?

Solution

We call the amount of chicken-food that one chicken eats per day a "portion". Let f be the number of "portions" of chicken-food that farmer Ankit has and let c be the number of chickens.

Normally, farmer Ankit would run out of chicken-food in f / c days.

If he would sell 75 of his chickens, he could feed the remaining chickens twenty days longer, so

$f / (c-75) = f / c + 20$

which can be rewritten to equation 1:

$20c^2 - 1500c - 75f = 0.$

If he would buy 100 extra chickens, he would run out of chicken-food fifteen days earlier, so

$f / (c+100) = f / c - 15$

which can be rewritten to equation 2:

$f = 3/20 \times c^2 + 15c$.

Combining equations 1 and 2 gives:

$20c^2 - 1500c - 75 \times (3/20 \times c^2 + 15c) = 0$.

Solving this equations gives $c=300$, so farmer Ankit has 300 chickens.

Another Question

One chicken lays two eggs in three days. How many eggs do three chickens lay in nine days?

Solution

1 chicken lays 2 eggs in 3 days, so 3 chickens lay 3×2=6 eggs in 3 days. In 9 days, these 3 chickens lay 3 times as much eggs as in 3 days. **Conclusion: 3 chickens lay 3×6=18 eggs in 9 days.**

Rowing Across the River

Kunal and Raj are on the two opposite banks of a river. They both have a rowing boat.

They both start off at the same time towards the opposite bank. They pass each other at 180 metres from the bank where Kunal departed. When reaching the opposite bank, they both take a rest for the same amount of time before they return. On the way back they pass each other at 100 metres from the bank from where Kunal returned.

Kunal and Raj both row with a constant speed, but Raj rows faster.

How wide is the river?

Solution

Call the requested width of the river *r*.

The first time that Kunal and Raj meet, the total distance which they have travelled together equals the width of the river, or *r*. The second time that Kunal and Raj meet, the total distance which they have travelled together equals twice the width of the river plus the width of the river, so 3 × *r*. Because Kunal and Raj row with a constant speed, it also holds that the distance which Kunal travelled in total at the second meeting, equals 3 times the distance which Kunal travelled in total at the first meeting.

The distance which Kunal travelled in total at the first meeting is 180. The distance which Kunal travelled in total at the second meeting is $r + 100$. When we combine the above we get the following equation:

$3 \times 180 = r + 100.$

When we solve this equation we find that $r = 440$.

Therefore, the river is 440 metres wide.

Beer and Bitterballs

On a nice summer day, two tourists visit the Dutch city of Gouda. During their tour through the center they spot a cosy terrace. They decide to have a drink and, as an appetizer, a portion of hot "bitterballs" (bitterballs are a Dutch delicacy, similar to croquettes). The waiter tells them that the bitterballs can be served in portions of 6, 9, or 20.

The Question: What is the largest number of bitterballs that cannot be ordered in these portions?

Solution

Every natural number is member of one of the following six series:

$$0, 6, 12, 18, \ldots$$
$$1, 7, 13, 19, \ldots$$
$$2, 8, 14, 20, \ldots$$
$$3, 9, 15, 21, \ldots$$
$$4, 10, 16, 22, \ldots$$
$$5, 11, 17, 23, \ldots$$

If for a number in one of these series holds that it can be made using the numbers 6, 9, and 20, then this also holds for all subsequent numbers in the series (by adding a multiple of 6).

To find out what the largest number is that cannot be made using the numbers 6, 9, and 20, we therefore only need to know, for every series, what the smallest number is that can be made in that way.

In the series 0, 6, 12, 18, ... the smallest number that can be made is 0, so there is no number that cannot be made.

In the series 1, 7, 13, 19, ... the smallest number that can be made is 49 (20+20+9), so 43 is the largest number that cannot be made.

In the series 2, 8, 14, 20, ... the smallest number that can be made is 20, so 14 is the largest number that cannot be made.

In the series 3, 9, 15, 21, ... the smallest number that can be made is 9, so 3 is the largest number that cannot be made.

In the series 4, 10, 16, 22, ... the smallest number that can be made is 40 (20+20), so 34 is the largest number that cannot be made.

In the series 5, 11, 17, 23, ... the smallest number that can be made is 29 (20+9), so 23 is the largest number that cannot be made.

Therefore, 43 is the largest number that cannot be made using the numbers 6, 9, and 20.

Speedy Sums

A salesman drives from Amsterdam to The Hague. The first half of the distance of his journey, he drives at a constant speed of 80 km/h. The second half of the distance of his journey, he drives at a constant speed of 120 km/h.

What is the salesman's average speed for the complete journey?

Solution

Let the length of the journey be *n* km. The first half of the journey takes $(1/2 \times n)/80 = 1/160 \times n$ hours, and the second half of the journey takes $(1/2 \times n)/120 = 1/240 \times n$ hours. The average speed for the complete journey is $n/(1/160 \times n + 1/240 \times n) = 96$ km/h.

Another Question

A race car driver drove, on a 4 km long race course, at an average speed of 120 km/h for the first 2 km. How fast does he have to go the second 2 km to average 240 km/h for the entire course?

Solution

At 120 km/h, it took the race car driver 1 minute to cover the first 2 km. To reach an average speed of 240 km/h for 4 km, that distance must be travelled in 1 minute. But that time was already used up in the first half of the course.

So the **Answer** is that, no matter how fast the race car drives in the second part of the course, it is impossible to average 240 km/h for the entire course!

Yet Another Question

Makkum and Stavoren are two villages. Manu and Donald want to go from Makkum to Stavoren. They leave at the same time. Manu goes by bicycle. Donald goes by car, which is six times as fast as Manu on his bicycle.

Unfortunately, Donald has a car breakdown half-way between Makkum and Stavoren. Fortunately, a passing farmer gives him a lift to Stavoren on his tractor. Unfortunately, the farmer drives only half as fast as Manu drives on his bicycle. Who of the two arrives first in Stavoren?

Solution

Because Donald travels the second part of the journey at half the speed at which Manu travels the whole journey, it takes Donald exactly as much time for the the second part the journey as it takes Manu for the whole journey. So, no matter how fast Donald is in the first part of the journey, Manu will arrive first in Stavoren.

The Fourth Question

Normally, the train between Utrecht and Amersfoort drives at an average speed of 90 km/h. One day, the train was delayed a little. Because of this, the average speed of the train between Utrecht and Amersfoort was only 70 km/h, and the train arrived four minutes late in Amersfoort. What is the distance between the stations of Utrecht and Amersfoort?

Solution

Let the distance between the stations of Utrecht and Amersfoort be d km. The four minutes delay is 4/60 part of an hour. Now the following holds:

$d / 90 + 4/60 = d / 70.$

Solving this equation gives $d=21$, so the distance between the stations of Utrecht and Amersfoort is 21 km.

Traveling Bird

Consider a road with two cars, at a distance of 100 kilometres, driving towards each other. The left car drives at a speed of forty kilometres per hour and the right car at a speed of sixty kilometres per hour. A bird starts at the same location as the right car and flies at a speed of 80 kilometres per hour. When it reaches the left car it turns its direction, and when it reaches the right car it turns its direction again to the opposite, etcetera.

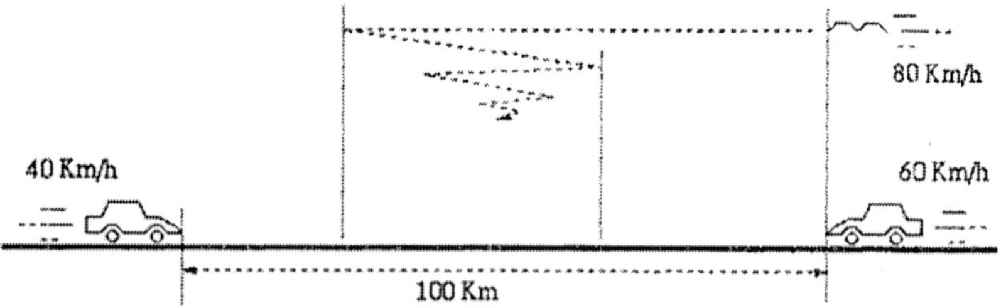

What is the total distance that the bird has travelled at the moment that the two cars have reached each other?

Solution

If you have written down a full paper of mathematical formulas, you haven't been thinking in the right direction.

It is obvious that the two cars meet each other after one hour. On that moment, the bird has flown for one hour.

Conclusion: The bird has flown 80 km/h × 1 h = 80 km.

Cork in the Canal

A swimmer jumps from a bridge over a canal and swims 1 kilometre stream up. After that first kilometre, he passes a floating cork. He continues swimming for half an hour and then turns around and swims back to the bridge.

The swimmer and the cork arrive at the bridge at the same time. The swimmer has been swimming with constant effort.

How fast does the water in the canal flow?

Solution

If you have written down a full paper of mathematical formulas, you have been thinking too complicated...

It is obvious that the cork does not move relatively to the water (i.e. has the same speed as the water). So if the swimmer is swimming away from the cork for half an hour (up stream), it will take him another half hour to swim back to the cork again. Because the swimmer is swimming with constant effort, his speed is constant relatively to the speed of the water.

You can look at it as if the water in the river doesn't move, the cork doesn't move, and the swimmer swims a certain time away from the cork and then back. So in that one hour time, the cork has floated from 1 kilometre up stream to the bridge.

Conclusion: The water in the canal flows at a speed of

1 km/h.

Square and Rectangle

The area of the square shown below is 8 × 8 = 64. The square is cut in the four parts A, B, C, and D, which are rearranged into the rectangle shown below. This rectangle has an area of

13 × 5 = 65.

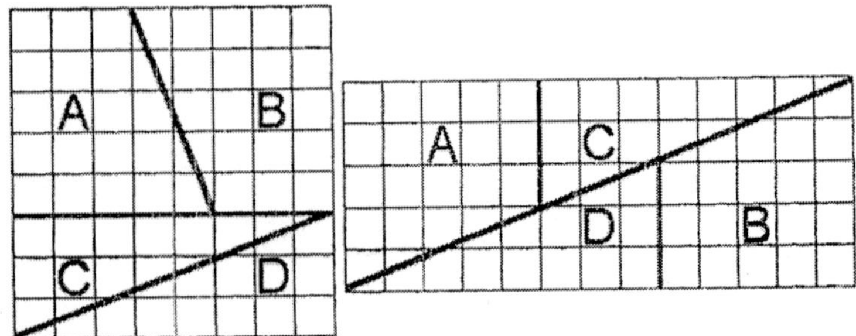

How can you explain the difference in area?

Solution

The picture of the rectangle is deceptive! The line XY shown in the picture of the rectangle (see below) is not a line at all. The parts XU and VY have a gradient of 2 / 5 = 0.4, and the parts XV and UY have a gradient of 3 / 8 = 0.375. So, in fact, XUYV is a parallellogram with an area of 1, not a line!

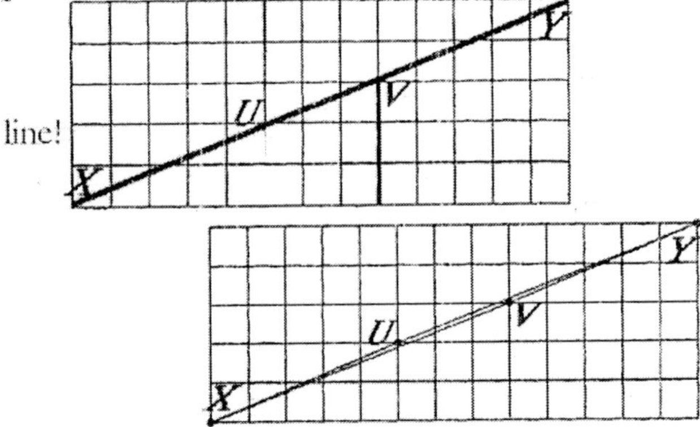

Three Taps

There is a water-cask with three different water-taps. With the smallest tap the water-cask can be filled in 20 minutes. With middle the tap the water-cask can be filled in 12 minutes. With the largest tap the water-cask can be filled in 5 minutes.

How long does it take to fill the water-cask with the three taps together?

Solution

The smallest tap fills 1/20 water-cask in 1 minute. The middle tap fills 1/12 water-cask in 1 minute. The largest tap fills 1/5 water-cask in 1 minute.

Together they fill $1/20 + 1/12 + 1/5 = 1/3$ water-cask in 1 minute. Therefore, the whole water-cask is filled in 3 minutes.

Notable Number

There is a unique number of ten digits, for which the following holds:

all digits from 0 up to 9 occur exactly once in the number;

the first digit is divisible by 1;

the number formed by the first two digits is divisible by 2;

the number formed by the first three digits is divisible by 3;

the number formed by the first four digits is divisible by 4;

the number formed by the first five digits is divisible by 5;

the number formed by the first six digits is divisible by 6;

the number formed by the first seven digits is divisible by 7;

the number formed by the first eight digits is divisible by 8;

the number formed by the first nine digits is divisible by 9;

the number formed by the ten digits is divisible by 10.

Which number is this?

Solution

We construct the number digit by digit.

Tenth digit

A number is divisible by 10 if it ends on a 0. Therefore, the tenth digit of the requested number must be a 0.

Fifth digit

A number is divisible by 5 if it ends on a 0 or 5. The 0 has already been used, so the fifth digit of the requested number is a 5.

First digit

A number is always divisible by 1. Nothing can be said about the first digit.

Second digit

A number is divisible by 2 if it is even, so if it ends on a 0, 2, 4, 6, or 8. The 0 has already been used, so the second digit of the requested number is a 2, 4, 6, or 8.

The fourth, sixth, and eighth digits of the requested number must also be divisible by two, so these digits must be 2, 4, 6, or 8 too. The digits on the first, third, fifth, seventh, and ninth positions of the requested number can only be 1, 3, 5, 7, or 9.

Third digit

A number is divisible by 3 if the sum of its digits is divisible by 3. Below all possibilities for the first thee digits of the requested number (first and third digits are 1, 3, 5, 7, or 9, second digit is 2, 4, 6, or 8, and the sum of the digits is divisible by 3):

123	723	147	183	783
129	729	741	189	789
321	921	369	381	981
327	927	963	387	987

Fourth digit

A number is divisible by 4 if:

the number ends on a 0, 4, or 8 and the last but one digit is even, or

the number ends on a 2 or 6 and the last but one digit is odd.

The third digit of the requested number is odd, so the fourth digit can only be a 2 or 6. Below are all possibilities for the first four digits of the requested number:

1236 9216 3692 3812 7892

1296	9276	9632	3816	7896
3216	1472	1832	3872	9812
3276	1476	1836	3876	9816

7236	7412	1892	7832	9872
7296	7416	1896	7836	9876

Sixth digit

A number is divisible by 6 if it is divisible by 2 and 3, so if it ends on a 0, 2, 4, 6, or 8, and the sum of the digits is divisible by 3. The first three digits of the requested number are already divisible by 3, so the sum of the fourth, fifth, and sixth digits must be divisible by 3 too. Below are the two possibilities for the fourth, fifth, and sixth digits of the requested number (fourth digit is 2, or 6, fifth digit is 5, sixth digit is 2, 4, 6, or 8, and the sum of the digits is divisible by 3):

258 654

Combined with what we already know about the first five digits, this gives the following possibilities for the first sixth digits of the requested number:

123654	723654	147258	183654	783654
129654	729654	741258	189654	789654
321654	921654	369258	381654	981654
327654	927654	963258	387654	987654

Eighth digit

A number is divisible by 8 if: the number formed by the last two digits is divisible by 8 and the last but two digit is even, or the number formed by the last two digits minus 4 is divisible by 8 and the last but two digit is odd.

The last but two digit is the sixth digit of the requested number, and is a 4 or 8. Therefore, the number formed by the seventh and eighth digits must be divisible by 8. In addition, we know that the seventh digit must be odd. These are the possible combinations:

16 32 56 72 96

Combined with what we already know about the first six digits, this gives the following possibilities for the first eight digits of the requested number:

18365472
18965432
18965472
38165472
14725896
74125896
78965432
98165432
98165472
98765432

Seventh digit

The number formed by the first seven digits of the requested number must be divisible by 7. For the numbers shown above, this only holds for the number 38165472.

Ninth digit

For the ninth digit, only the digit 9 remains. Note that every number formed by the digits 1 up to 9 is divisible by 9. A number is divisible by 9 if the sum of its digits is divisible by 9. The sum of the digits 1 up to 9 is 45, which is divisible by 9.

Conclusion

The requested number is 3816547290.

Another Question

There is a unique number of which the square and the cube together use all digits from 0 up to 9 exactly once. Which number is this?

Solution

The number is 69: 692 = 4761 and 693 = 328509.

Baffling Birthdays

In Mrs. Madhuri's class are twenty-six children. None of the children was born on February 29th.

What is the probability that at least two children have their birthdays on the same day?

Solution

The probability that at least two children have their birthdays on the same day, is 1 minus the probability that all children have their birthdays on different days. Therefore, we first calculate the latter probability.

None of the children was born on the 29th of February, so there are 365 days on which each child could have its birthday. The first child can have its birthday on any day (probability 1). The second child must have his its birthday on a different day than the first child; the probability for that is 364/365. The third child has to have its birthday on again a different day than the first and second; the probability for that is 363/365. Continue like this till the 26th child with a probability of 340/365. The total probability then becomes 1 × 364/365 × 363/365 × ... × 340/365 (about 40 per cent).

The probability that at least two children have their birthdays on the same day, is 1 minus above-mentioned probability, around 60 per cent.

The Prince and the Pearls

Long ago, a young Chinese prince wanted to marry a Mandarin's daughter. The Mandarin decided to test the prince. He gave the prince two empty, porcelain vases, 100 white pearls, and 100 black pearls. "You must put all the pearls in the vases", he told the prince. "After this, I will call my daughter from the room next door. She will take a random pearl from one of the two vases. If this pearl is a black one, you are allowed to marry my daughter."

What was the best way in which the prince could divide the pearls over the vases?

Solution

The best way is to put one black pearl in the first vase, and all other pearls in the second vase. Then, the probability of grabbing a black pearl from the first vase is 1, and the probability of grabbing a black pearl from the second vase is 99/199. The total probability of grabbing a black pearl is 0.5 × 1 + 0.5 × 99/199 = 298/398 (approximately 74.9%).

Another Question

You have three vases: one vase containing two white pearls, one vase containing one white and one black pearl, and one vase containing two black pearls. From one of these vases, a pearl is taken. This pearl turns out to be white. What is the probability that the other pearl in the same vase is also white?

Solution

There are three pearls that can be the white pearl that was taken from the chosen vase:

The first pearl from the vase with two white pearls: in this case, the other pearl is also white.

The second pearl from the vase with two white pearls: in this case, the other pearl is also white.

The white pearl from the vase with one white and one black pearl: in this case, the other pearl is black.

The probability that the other pearl in the same vase is also white, is therefore 2/3.

Yet Another Question

You have ten vases. Five of the vases contain a white pearl and four of the vases contain a black pearl (note that a vase may contain both a white and a black pearl!). You randomly select one of the ten vases. What is the probability that the vase you chose is empty?

Solution

The probability that the chosen vase does not contain a white pearl is (10-5)/10 = 1/2. The probability that the chosen vase does not contain a black pearl is (10-4)/10 = 3/5. The probability that the chosen vase does not contain any pearl is therefore 1/2 × 3/5 = 3/10 (which is 30%).

Plus and Minus

Below is an equation that isn't correct yet. By adding a number of plus signs and minus signs between the digits on the left side (without changes the order of the digits), the equation can be made correct.

123456789 = 100

How many different ways are there to make the equation correct?

Solution

There are 11 different ways:

123+45-67+8-9 = 100

123+4-5+67-89 = 100

123-45-67+89 = 100

123-4-5-6-7+8-9 = 100

12+3+4+5-6-7+89 = 100

12+3-4+5+67+8+9 = 100

12-3-4+5-6+7+89 = 100

1+23-4+56+7+8+9 = 100

1+23-4+5+6+78-9 = 100

1+2+34-5+67-8+9 = 100

1+2+3-4+5+6+78+9 = 100

Remark: If it is not only allowed to put plus signs and minus signs between the digits, but also in front of the first 1, then there is a twelfth possibility: -1+2-3+4+5+6+78+9=100.

Missing Pages

From a book, a number of consecutive pages are missing. The sum of the page numbers of these pages is 9808.

Which pages are missing?

Solution

Let the number of missing pages be n and the first missing page $p+1$. Then the pages $p+1$ up to and including $p+n$ are missing, and n times the average of the numbers of the missing pages must be equal to 9808:

$n\times(((p+1)+(p+n))/2) = 9808$

In other words:

$n\times(2\times p+n+1)/2 = 2\times2\times2\times2\times613$

So:

$n\times(2\times p+n+1) = 2\times2\times2\times2\times2\times613$

One of the two terms n and $2\times p+n+1$ must be even, and the other one must be odd. Moreover, the term n must be smaller than the term $2\times p+n+1$. It follows that there are only two solutions:

$n=1$ and $2\times p+n+1=2\times2\times2\times2\times2\times613$, so $n=1$ and $p=9808$, so only page 9808 is missing.

$n=2\times2\times2\times2\times2$ and $2\times p+n+1=613$, so $n=32$ and $p=290$, so the pages 291 up to and including 322 are missing.

Because it is asked which pages (plural) are missing, the solution is: the pages 291 up to and including 322 are missing.

All Apples

On the market, Mrs. Geeta and Mrs. Sunita sell apples. Mrs. Geeta sells her apples per two for 0.50 Rs. The apples of Mrs. Sunita are a bit smaller; she sells hers per three for 0.50 Rs. At a certain moment, when both ladies have the same amount of apples left, Mrs. Sunita is being called away. She asks her neighbour to take care of her goods. To make everything not too complicated, Mrs. Geeta puts all apples to one big pile, and starts selling them for one Rs. per five apples. When Mrs. Sunita returns at the end of the day, all apples have been sold. But when they start dividing the money, there appears to be a shortage of 3.50 Rs.

Supposing they divide the amount of money equally, how much does Mrs. Geeta lose with this deal?

Solution

The big pile of apples contains the same amount of large apples of a quarter of a Rs. each (from Mrs. Geeta), as smaller apples of one sixth Rs. each (from Mrs. Sunita). The average price is therefore (1/4 + 1/6) / 2 = 5/24 Rs. But the apples are sold for 1/5 Rs. each (5 apples for 1 Rs.).

This means that per sold apple there is a shortage of 5/24 -

1/5 = 1/120 Rs. The total shortage is 3.50 Rs., so the ladies together started out with 420 apples. These are worth 1/5 × 420 = 84 Rs., or with equal division 42 Rs. for each. If Mrs. Geeta would have sold her 210 apples herself, she would have received 52.50 Rs.

Conclusion: Mrs. Geeta loses 10.50 Rs. in this deal.

Buying Books

Two friends, Anita and Gaurav, go to a bookshop, together with their sons Pankaj and Harsh. All four of them buy some books; each book costs a whole amount in shillings. When they leave the bookshop, they notice that both fathers have spent 21 shillings more than their respective sons.

Moreover, each of them paid per book the same amount of shillings as books that he bought. The difference between the number of books of Anita and Pankaj is five.

Who is the father of Harsh?

Solution

For each father-son couple holds: the father bought x books of x shillings, the son bought y books of y shillings. The difference between their expenses is 21 shillings, thus $x^2 - y^2 = 21$.

Since x and y are whole numbers (each book costs a whole amount of shillings), there are two possible solutions: (x=5, y=2) or (x=11, y−10).

Because the difference between Anita and Pankaj is 5 books, this means that father Anita bought 5 books and son Pankaj 10. This means that the other son, Harsh, bought 2 books, and that his father is Anita.

Four Flies

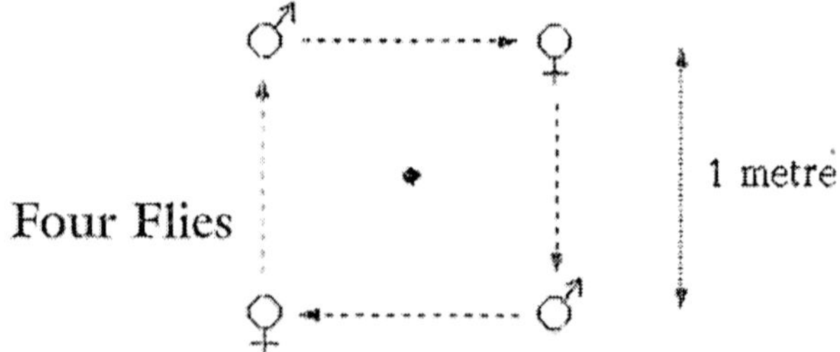

Consider 4 (dimensionless) flies, 2 males and 2 females. They are situated at the corners of 1 square metre. Every fly tries to reach the male/female fly in front of her/him. Their initial situation is visualized in the picture. Since the flies are flying towards another, they will meet each other at a certain time in the center of the square.

What is the length of the path they have travelled at the moment they reach each other?

Solution

Because all flies constantly fly perpendicular to another fly, they all travel the shortest distance to each other, which is 1 metre (all flies make a kind of spiral flight to the centre of the square, and during this flight, the flies constantly form a square until they meet in the centre).

Conclusion: The flies all travel 1 metre.

Circling Cyclist

A cyclist drove one kilometre, with the wind in his back, in three minutes and drove the same way back, against the wind in four minutes.

If we assume that the cyclist always puts constant force on the pedals, how much time would it take him to drive one kilometre without wind?

Solution

The cyclist drives one kilometre in three minutes with the wind in his back, so in four minutes he drives 1 1/3 kilometre. Against the wind, he drives 1 kilometre in four minutes. If the wind helps the cyclist during four minutes and hinders the cyclist during another four minutes, then – in these eight minutes – the cyclist drives 2 1/3 kilometres. Without wind, he would also drive 2 1/3 kilometres in eight minutes and his average speed would then be 17.5 kilometres per hour. So it will take him 3 3/7 minutes to drive one kilometre.

Odd Oranges

Greengrocer C. Carrot wants to expose his oranges neatly for sale. Doing this he discovers that one orange is left over when he places them in groups of three. The same happens if he tries to place them in groups of 5, 7, or 9 oranges. Only when he makes groups of 11 oranges, it fits exactly.

How many oranges does the greengrocer have at least?

Solution

Assume the number of oranges is A. Then A-1 is divisible by 3, 5, 7 and 9. So, A-1 is a multiple of $5 \times 7 \times 9 = 315$ (Note: 9 is also a multiple of 3, so 3 must not be included!). We are looking for a value of N for which holds that $315 \times N + 1$ is divisible by 11. After some trying it turns out that the smallest N for which this holds is N = 3. This means that the greengrocer has at least 946 oranges.

Note that for N = 14, 25, 36, etc. (so each time 11 more) it also holds that $315 \times N + 1$ is divisible by 11.

Water Bucket

Calculate the minimum outside surface of a cylindrical bucket with an open upper side and which can hold 30 litres of water.

What is the minimum outside surface?

Solution

The surface of a cylinder with an open upper side is: O = $pi \times R^2 + 2 \times pi \times R3H$, where R is the radius of the cylinder and H is the height. The volume is given, V = 30 = $pi \times R^2 \times H$ litres (or dm³). The surface can then be written as $O = pi \times R^2 + 2 \times V/R$. If you take the first derivative of R and look where this derivative equals 0 you get $R_{min} = (V/pi)1/3$. So the minimum surface is $O = pi \times R_{min}^2 + 2 \times pi \times R_{min} \times H = 3 \times pi 1/3 \times V^2/3$ or about 42,42 dm².

The Cucumber Case

On a sunny morning, a greengrocer places 200 kilograms of cucumbers in cases in front of his shop. At that moment, the cucumbers are 99% water. In the afternoon, it turns out that it is the hottest day of the year, and as a result, the cucumbers dry out a little bit. At the end of the day, the greengrocer has not sold a single cucumber, and the cucumbers are only 98% water.

How many kilograms of cucumbers has the greengrocer left at the end of the day?

Solution

In the morning, the 200 kilograms of cucumbers are 99% water. So the non-water part of the cucumbers has a mass of 2 kilograms. At the end of the day, the cucumbers are 98% water. The remaining 2% is still the 2 kilograms of non-water material (which does not change when the water evaporates).

If 2% equals 2 kilograms, then 100% equals 100 kilograms. So, the greengrocer has 100 kilograms of cucumbers left at the end of the day.

Escalator Exercise

You walk upwards on an escalator, with a speed of 1 step per second. After 50 steps you are at the end. You turn around and run downwards with a speed of 5 steps per second. After 125 steps you are back at the beginning of the escalator.

How many steps do you need if the escalator stands still?

Solution

Let v be the speed of the escalator, in steps per second. Let L be the number of steps that you need to take when the escalator stands still.

Upwards (along with the escalator), you walk 1 step per second. You need 50 steps, so that takes 50 seconds. This gives the following equation:

L steps - 50 seconds × v steps/second = 50 steps.

Downwards (against the direction of the escalator), you walk 5 steps per second. You need 125 steps, so that takes 25 seconds. This gives the following equation:

L steps + 25 seconds × v steps/second = 125 steps.

From the two equations follows: L = 100, v = 1. When the escalator stands still, you need 100 steps.

Chapter 4

General Riddles

It is greater than God and more evil than the devil. The poor have it, the rich need it and if you eat it you'll die. What is it?

Answer: Nothing. Nothing is greater than God, nothing is more evil than the devil, the poor have nothing, the rich need nothing and if you eat nothing you'll die.

ꕥ

It walks on four legs in the morning, two legs at noon and three legs in the evening. What is it?

Answer: Man (or woman). Crawls on all fours as a baby, walks on two legs as an adult and uses two legs and a cane when they're old.

ꕥ

I am the beginning of the end, and the end of time and space. I am essential to creation, and I surround every place. What am I?

Answer: The letter e. End, timE, spacE, Every placE.

ꕥ

What always runs but never walks, often murmurs, never talks, has a bed but never sleeps, has a mouth but never eats?

Answer: A river.

ଔଷ

I never was, am always to be. No one ever saw me, nor ever will. And yet I am the confidence of all, To live and breath on this terrestrial ball. What am I?

Answer: Tomorrow or the future.

ଔଷ

There was a green house. Inside the green house there was a white house. Inside the white house there was a red house. Inside the red house there were lots of babies. What is it?

Answer: A watermelon.

ଔଷ

What is in seasons, seconds, centuries and minutes but not in decades, years or days?

Answer: The letter 'n'.

ଔଷ

Think of words ending in -GRY. Angry and hungry are two of them. There are only three words in the English language. What is the third word? The word is something that everyone uses every day. If you have listened carefully, I have already told you what it is.

Answer: It states, "There are only three words in the English language. What is the third word?" The third word of that phrase is of course "language." Don't get angry at me, I didn't make it up.

ଔଷ

The one who makes it, sells it. The one who buys it, never uses it. The one that uses it never knows that he's using it. What is it?

Answer: A coffin.

ଔଷ

The more you have of it, the less you see. What is it?

Answer: Darkness.

ଔଷ

What has a head, a tail, is brown, and has no legs?

Answer: A penny.

ᴓᴕ

What English word has three consecutive double letters?

Answer: Bookkeeper.

ᴓᴕ

What's black when you get it, red when you use it, and white when you're all through with it?

Answer: Charcoal.

ᴓᴕ

You throw away the outside and cook the inside. Then you eat the outside and throw away the inside. What did you eat?

Answer: An ear of corn.

ᴓᴕ

I am always hungry,

I must always be fed,

The finger I touch,

Will soon turn red.

Answer: Fire.

ᴓᴕ

Ripped from my mother's womb,

Beaten and burned,

I become a blood thirsty killer.

What am I?

Answer: Iron ore.

ᴓᴕ

I know a word of letters three. Add two, and fewer there will be.

Answer: Few.

ᴓᴕ

I give you a group of three. One is sitting down, and will never get up. The second eats as much as is given to him, yet is always hungry. The third goes away and never returns.

Answer: Stove, fire, smoke.

ଓଃ

I have four legs but no tail. Usually I am heard only at night. What am I?

Answer: A frog. The frog is an amphibian in the order Anura (meaning "tail-less") and usually makes noises at night during its mating season.

ଓଃ

Half-way up the hill, I see thee at last, lying beneath me with thy sounds and sights — A city in the twilight, dim and vast, with smoking roofs, soft bells, and gleaming lights.

Answer: The past. (Longfellow).

ଓଃ

When young, I am sweet in the sun.

When middle-aged, I make you gay.

When old, I am valued more than ever.

Answer: Wine.

ଓଃ

If you break me

I do not stop working,

If you touch me

I may be snared,

If you lose me

Nothing will matter.

Answer: Your heart.

ଓଃ

All about, but cannot be seen,

Can be captured, cannot be held,

No throat, but can be heard.

Answer: Wind.

ଓଃଃ

Until I am measured
I am not known,
Yet how you miss me
When I have flown.

Answer: Time.

ଓଃଃ

I drive men mad
For love of me,
Easily beaten,
Never free.

Answer: Gold.

ଓଃଃ

When set loose
I fly away,
Never so cursed
As when I go astray.

Answer: A fart.

ଓଃଃ

Lighter than what
I am made of,
More of me is hidden
Than is seen.

Answer: Iceberg.

ଓଃଃ

Each morning I appear
To lie at your feet,
All day I will follow

No matter how fast you run,
Yet I nearly perish
In the midday sun.
Answer: Shadow.

ଔ

My life can be measured in hours,
I serve by being devoured.
Thin, I am quick
Fat, I am slow
Wind is my foe.
Answer: A candle.

ଔ

I am seen in the water
If seen in the sky,
I am in the rainbow,
A jay's feather,
And lapis lazuli.
Answer: Blue.

ଔ

Glittering points
That downward thrust,
Sparkling spears
That never rust.
Answer: Icicle.

ଔ

You heard me before,
Yet you hear me again,
Then I die,
'Till you call me again.
Answer: An echo.

Three lives have I.
Gentle enough to soothe the skin,
Light enough to caress the sky,
Hard enough to crack rocks.
Answer: Water.

At the sound of me, men may dream
Or stamp their feet
At the sound of me, women may laugh
Or sometimes weep
Answer: Music.

What does man love more than life
Fear more than death or mortal strife
What the poor have, the rich require,
and what contented men desire,
What the miser spends and the spendthrift saves
And all men carry to their graves?
Answer: Nothing.

I build up castles.
I tear down mountains.
I make some men blind,
I help others to see.
What am I?
Answer: Sand.

Two in a corner,
1 in a room,

0 in a house, but 1 in a shelter. What am I?

Answer: The letter r.

ᘓᘎ

Five hundred begins it, five hundred ends it,

Five in the middle is seen;

First of all figures, the first of all letters,

Take up their stations between.

Join all together, and then you will bring

Before you the name of an eminent king.

Answer: DAVID (Roman numerals).

ᘓᘎ

At night they come without being fetched. By day they are lost without being stolen. What are they?

Answer: The stars.

ᘓᘎ

It cannot be seen, it weighs nothing, but when put into a barrel, it makes it lighter. What is it?

Answer: A hole.

ᘓᘎ

How far will a blind dog walk into a forest?

Answer: Halfway. After he gets halfway, he's walking out of the forest.

ᘓᘎ

What happens when you throw a yellow rock into a purple stream?

Answer: It makes a splash.

ᘓᘎ

What starts with a T, ends with a T, and has T in it?

Answer: A teapot.

ᘓᘎ

As I went over London Bridge

I met my sister Jenny

I broke her neck and drank her blood
And left her standing empty
Answer: A bottle of gin.

☙

Whoever makes it, tells it not.
Whoever takes it, knows it not.
Whoever knows it, wants it not
Answer: Counterfeit money.

☙

I am, in truth, a yellow fork
From tables in the sky
By inadvertent fingers dropped
The awful cutlery.
Of mansions never quite disclosed
And never quite concealed
The apparatus of the dark
To ignorance revealed.
Answer: Lightning.

☙

You saw me where I never was and where I could not be. And yet within that very place, my face you often see. What am I?
Answer: A reflection.

☙

I turn polar bears white
and I will make you cry.
I make guys have to pee
and girls comb their hair.
I make celebrities look stupid
and normal people look like celebrities.
I turn pancakes brown

and make your champagne bubble.

If you squeeze me, I'll pop.

If you look at me, you'll pop.

Can you guess the riddle?

Answer: The **Answer** to this admittedly lame riddle is, "No." The reason is that the question at the very end asks if you can guess the riddle and there is nothing that satisfies the requirements above.

☙❧

Say my name and I disappear. What am I?

Answer: Silence.

☙❧

What is it that after you take away the whole, some still remains?

Answer: Wholesome.

☙❧

A box without hinges, lock or key, yet golden treasure lies within. What is it?

Answer: An egg.

☙❧

Forward I'm heavy, but backwards I'm not. What am I?

Answer: Ton.

☙❧

I can be long, or I can be short.

I can be grown, and I can be bought.

I can be painted, or left bare.

I can be round, or square.

What am I?

Answer: A fingernail.

☙❧

Why doesn't a mountain covered with snow catch cold?

Answer: Because it has a snowcap.

☙❧

One by one we fall from heaven
down into the depths of past
And our world is ever upturned
so that yet some time we'll last
Answer: Sands in an hourglass.

ꕥ

I drift forever with the current
down these long canals they've made
Tame, yet wild, I run elusive
Multitasking to your aid.
Before I came, the world was darker
Colder, sometimes, rougher, true
But though I might make living easy,
I'm good at killing people too.
Answer: Electricity (or lightning).

ꕥ

Reaching stiffly for the sky,
I bare my fingers when it's cold
In warmth I wear an emerald glove
And in between I dress in gold
Answer: A deciduous tree.

ꕥ

Kings and queens may cling to power
and the jester's got his call
But, as you may all discover,
the common one outranks them all
Answer: An ace (in a deck of cards).

ꕥ

Every dawn begins with me
At dusk I'll be the first you see

And daybreak couldn't come without
What midday centers all about
Daises grow from me, I'm told
And when I come, I end all cold
But in the sun I won't be found
Yet still, each day I'll be around

Answer: The letter d.

ᏡᏕᏑ

Kings and lords and Christians raised them
Since they stand for higher powers
Yet few of them would stand, I'm certain,
if women ruled this world of ours

Answer: A tower.

ᏡᏕᏑ

Soft and fragile is my skin
I get my growth in mud
I'm dangerous as much as pretty
For if not careful, I draw blood.

Answer: A thorn.

ᏡᏕᏑ

Three brothers share a family sport:
A non-stop marathon
The oldest one is fat and short
And trudges slowly on
The middle brother's tall and slim
And keeps a steady pace
The youngest runs just like the wind,
A-speeding through the race
"He's young in years, we let him run,"

The other brothers say
"Cause though he's surely number one,
He's second, in a way."

Answer: The hands on a clock (hour, minute, second).

ꕥ

It's true I bring serenity,
And hang around the stars
But yet I live in misery;
You'll find me behind bars
With thieves and villains I consort
In prison I'll be found
But I would never go to court,
Unless there's more than one

Answer: The letter s.

ꕥ

I am a box that holds keys without locks, yet they can unlock your soul. What am I?

Answer: A piano.

ꕥ

There once was a strange man who loved wordplay, he had a very important and successful business that would take insect shipments from all across the world and distribute them to zoos across the US.

What was the name of his company?

Answer: ImportANT.

ꕥ

There is one word that stands the test of time and holds fast to the center of everything. Though everyone will try at least once in their life to move around this word, but in fact, unknowingly, they use it every moment of the day. Young or old, awake or in sleep, human or animal, this word stands fast. It belongs to everyone, to all living things, but no one can master it. The word is?

Answer: Gravity.

ꕥ

My days are in the summer
When you'll eat me when I'm hot
In fact I'll even eat myself
Where battles tough are fought
But when you find me in a fight
'Twill be high in the sky
And if you catch me napping
I suggest you let me lie
When you're bad come to my house
From Ma get thoughts profound
Am I big or am I small?
Some say I'm just a pound.

Answer: Dog. Dog days, hot dog, dog pound, dog fight.

ꕥ

My first is twice in apple but not once in tart. My second is in liver but not in heart. My third is in giant and also in ghost. Whole I'm best when I am roast. What am I?

Answer: A pig.

ꕥ

What gets wetter as it dries?

Answer: A towel.

ꕥ

This is a most unusual paragraph. How quickly can you find out what is so unusual about it? It looks so ordinary you'd think nothing was wrong with it – and in fact, nothing is wrong with it. It is unusual though. Why? Study it, think about it, and you may find out. Try to do it without coaching. If you work at it for a bit it will dawn on you. So jump to it and try your skill at figuring it out.

Good luck - don't blow your cool!

Answer: The most common letter in the English language, the letter e, is not found in the entire paragraph.

ଓଃଌ

When you went into the woods you got me.

You hated me yet you wanted to find me.

You went home with me cause you couldn't find me

What was it?

Answer: A splinter.

ଓଃଌ

An iron horse with a flaxen tail.

The faster the horse runs,

the shorter his tail becomes.

What is it?

Answer: A needle and thread.

ଓଃଌ

You have to travel far before you turn it over. What is it?

Answer: An odometre.

A mile from end to end, yet as close to as a friend. A precious commodity, freely given. Seen on the dead and on the living. Found on the rich, poor, short and tall, but shared among children most of all. What is it?

Answer: A smile.

ଓଃଌ

I'm full of holes, yet I'm full of water. What am I?

Answer: A sponge.

ଓଃଌ

Four of us are in your field

But our differences keep us at yield

ଓଃଌ

First, a one that is no fool

Though he resembles a gardener's tool.

ଓଃ

Next, one difficult to split in two

And a girl once had one as big as her shoe.

ଓଃ

Then, to the mind, one's a lovely bonder

And truancy makes it grow fonder.

ଓଃ

Last, a stem connecting dots of three

Knowing all this, what are we?

Answer: The four suits in a deck of standard playing cards.

ଓଃ

The Spade is a gardener's tool.

The Diamond is the hardest gem to break. "Little Girl and Queen" is a Mother Goose rhyme, in which the Queen gave the girl a large diamond for picking the Queen some roses.

The Heart bonds with the mind to form love. Absence makes the heart grow fonder.

The Club, or Clover, is three dots connected around a stem.

ଓଃ

I am a word of meanings three.

Three ways of spelling me there be.

The first is an odour. a smell if you will.

The second some money, but not in a bill.

The third is past tense, a method of passing things on or around.

ଓଃ

Can you tell me now, what these words are, that have the same sound?

Answer: Scent, cent, sent.

ଓଃ

It's red, blue, purple and green, no one can reach it, not even the queen. What is it?

Answer: A rainbow.

ଔଓ

What question can you never honestly **Answer** yes to?

Answer: Are you asleep? (or dead)

ଔଓ

What has a neck and no head, two arms but no hands?

Answer: A shirt (or sweater, Arunet etc.)

ଔଓ

I live in water

If you cut my head I'm at your door,

If you cut my tail I'm fruit,

If you cut both I'm with you

What am I?

Answer: A pearl. They're found underwater. Removing the head (p) leaves Earl, a guy who could be at your door. Removing the tail (l) leaves pear, a fruit and if you cut both off you're left with ear, which is with you because it's attached to your head.

ଔଓ

Feed me and I live, give me drink and I die. What am I?

Answer: Fire.

ଔଓ

What begins and has no end? What is the ending of all that begins?

Answer: Death or decay.

ଔଓ

A man went to the hardware store to buy items for his house.

1 would cost 25 Rs.

12 would cost 50 Rs.

122 would cost 75 Rs.

When he left the store he had spent $.75, what did he buy?

Answer: House numbers.

ʚɞ

What makes a loud noise when changing its Arunet, becomes larger but weighs less?

Answer: Popcorn.

ʚɞ

The more you take, the more you leave behind.

Answer: Footsteps.

ʚɞ

I am a word of 5 letters and people eat me. If you remove the first letter I become a form of energy. Remove the first two and I'm needed to live. Scramble the last 3 and you can drink me. What am I?

Answer: wheat.

heat

eat

tea

ʚɞ

Before any changes I'm a garlic or spice. My first is altered and I'm a hand-warming device. My second is changed and I'm trees in full bloom. The next letter change makes a deathly old Tomb. Change the fourth to make a fruit of the vine. Change the last for a chart plotted with lines. What was I? What did I become? What did I turn out to be?

Answer: clove

glove

grove

grave

grape

graph

ʚɞ

A woman shoots her husband, then holds him under water for five minutes. Finally, she hangs him. Five minutes later they enjoy a wonderful dinner together. How can this be?

Answer: She took a photo of him and developed it in the dark room.

ଔ

Remove six letters from this sequence to reveal a familiar English word. BSAINXLEATNTEARS

Answer: BANANA (Removed SIX LETTERS)

ଔ

Alive without breath,

As cold as death,

Clad in mail never clinking,

Never thirsty, ever drinking

Answer: A fish.

ଔ

I can always go up, never down,

I can always turn left, never right,

I am always hot when I'm cold

Answer: A ski lift.

ଔ

A cowboy rides into town on Friday, stays for three days and leaves on Friday. How did he do it?

Answer: The horse's name is Friday.

ଔ

I'm lighter than air but a million men can't lift me. What am I?

Answer: A bubble.

ଔ

What has roots that nobody sees,

Is taller than trees,

Up, up it goes,

Yet it never grows?

Answer: A mountain.

ᴕᴕ

This thing all things devours,

Birds, beasts, trees, and flowers.

Gnaws iron bites steel,

Grinds hard stones to meal,

Slays king, ruins town,

And beats high mountain down

Answer: time.

ᴕᴕ

It cannot be seen, it cannot be felt,

Cannot be heard, cannot be smelt,

Lies behind stars and under hills,

And empty holes it fills.

Comes first follows after,

Ends life kills laughter.

Answer: Darkness.

ᴕᴕ

An eye in a blue face

Saw an eye in a green face.

'That eye is like this eye'

Said the first eye,

But in a low, not high place.

Answer: The sun shining on daisies.

ᴕᴕ

Two words is my answer. In order to keep me, you have to give me. What am I?

Answer: Your word.

ᴕᴕ

A man is born in 1946 and dies in 1947, yet he was 86 years old. How is that possible?

Answer: He was born in room #1946 of the hospital when he was born, and died in room #1947 86 years later.

☙❧

I go in hard.

I come out soft.

You blow me hard.

What am I?

Answer: Gum.

☙❧

If you drop me I'm sure to crack but give me a smile and I'll always smile back.

Answer: A mirror.

☙❧

What does this represent?

Standing

World

Answer: Standing on top of the world.

☙❧

Old Mother Twitchet had one eye

and a long tail that she let fly.

And every time she went through a gap,

she left some tail in the trap.

Answer: A needle and thread.

☙❧

Little Miss Eticote

In her white petticoat

And her red nose

The longer she stands

The shorter she grows.

Answer: A candle.

ଓଃଃଚ

Only one colour, but not one size,
stuck at the bottom , yet easily flies;
present in sun, but not in rain;
doing no harm, and feeling no pain.

Answer: A shadow.

ଓଃଃଚ

What force and strength cannot get through,
I, with a gentle touch, can do.
And many in the street would stand,
were I not a friend at hand.

Answer: A key.

ଓଃଃଚ

Round like an apple, deep like a cup,
yet all the king's horses cannot pull it up.

Answer: A well.

ଓଃଃଚ

Thirty white horses on a red hill,
first champ, then stamp, and then stand still.

Answer: Your mouth while chewing.

ଓଃଃଚ

Black we are and much admired,
men seek us if they are tired,
We tire the horse, comfort man,
guess this riddle if you can.

Answer: Coal.

ଓଃଃଚ

Weight in my belly;

trees on my back;

nails in my ribs;

feet I do lack.

Answer: A ship.

ଔଡ଼

What holds two people together but touches only one?

Answer: A wedding ring (at least it used to).

ଔଡ଼

What lives in the corner but travels the world?

Answer: A postage stamp.

ଔଡ଼

I'm white, I'm round, but not always around. Sometimes you see me, sometimes you don't. What am I?

Answer: The moon.

ଔଡ଼

There are two meanings to me. With one I may need to be broken, with the other I hold on. My favourite characteristic is my charming dimple. What am I?

Answer: A tie.

ଔଡ଼

Toss me out of the window,

You'll find a grieving wife,

Pull me back but through the door, and

Watch someone give life!

What am I?

Answer: The letter 'n' (widow, donor).

ଔଡ଼

What has a head, one arm, one leg and a round bottom?

Answer: A handicapped parking sign.

ଔଡ଼

I go in dry and come out wet, The longer I'm in, the stronger I get. What am I?

Answer: A tea bag.

ଓଃ୭ଠ

In the day I stand tall in a white petticoat. By evening I'm in my short black dress. What am I?

Answer: The wick of a candle.

ଓଃ୭ଠ

I cannot be other than what I am

Until the man who made me dies

Power and glory will fall to me finally

Only when he last closes his eyes.

Answer: A prince.

ଓଃ୭ଠ

Two in a whole and four in a pair

And six in a trio you see

And eight's a quartet but what you must get

Is the name that fits just one of me?

Answer: A half.

ଓଃ୭ଠ

One am I, among six others:

Largest, smallest,

Cold, dark

and two brothers.

Who am I?

Answer: Europe (The Seven continents).

ଓଃ୭ଠ

What asks no questions but receives lots of answers?

Answer: A phone or doorbell

ଓଃ୭ଠ

In the night a mountain in the morning a meadow. What am I?

Answer: A bed.

ᴓ

What goes up but never comes down?

Answer: Your age.

ᴓ

I have an end but no beginning, a home but no family, a space without room. I never speak but there is no word I cannot make. What am I?

Answer: A keyboard.

ᴓ

Three little letters

A paradox to some.

The worse that it is

The better it becomes.

Answer: Pun.

ᴓ

I am in a house with no doors. There are people inside but no reply. Who am I?

Answer: A fish.

ᴓ

I hide but my head is outside. What am I?

Answer: A nail.

ᴓ

What three letter English word has an odd start, an even finish and an infinitely long middle?

Answer: The word vex. "v" is Roman numeral 5, which is odd. "x" is Roman numeral 10, which is even. "e" is the base of the natural logarithm and is irrational (e = 2.718281828...). Its mantissa (the part to the right of the decimal point) is infinitely long.

■■■

Chapter 5

Harder Riddles

I help all living things to survive. I give shade to others. People use me for their various needs. I have rings to determine my age. Who am I?

Answer: Tree.

ଔଓ

Place the following letters in such a manner that it becomes something which is used to clean:

boas

Answer: soap (flip the alphabet b so that it becomes p).

ଔଓ

I am fair and shiny. People use me to find how hot they are. Some call me God. Who am I?

Answer: Mercury.

ଔଓ

When can you make the following equation correct?

14+1=3

Answer: In a clock when we add 14 hrs and 1 hr we get 15 hrs i.e. 3 o'clock.

ଔଓ

I am a seven letter word. I have two sets of double letters in a row. I can fly like a bird or a plane. Kids love me. I end with N. Who am I?

Answer: Balloon.

ଔଓ

I am clean when I look black and dirty when I look white. Who am I?

Answer: Blackboard.

ଔଓ

I run around a house but I don't move. Who am I?

Answer: Fence.

ଔଓ

I am an English word. I have three consecutive double letters. Who am I?

Answer: Bookkeeper.

ଔଓ

I have wheels and flies. But I don't have any wings. Who am I?

Answer: Garbage truck.

ଔଓ

I am a 7 letter word. I become longer when my third letter is removed. Who am I?

Answer: Lounger.

ଔଓ

I have a tongue but I can't talk. I have no legs or wings but I can move from one place to another. Who am I?

Answer: A shoe.

ଔଓ

I am an eight letter word. My first four letters combine to form an atmospheric state. My third, fourth, fifth, sixth and seventh letters give support. My last three letters is the name of a person. Who am I?

Answer: MISTAKEN.

ঔ

Spell eighty using only two alphabets.

Answer: A-T.

ঔ

Where does Friday comes before Thursday?

Answer: In the dictionary.

ঔ

I am a 5 letter word. Take away my first and last letter, I will remain same. If you also take away my middle letter, I will remain same. Who am I?

Answer: EMPTY.

ঔ

You can find me in the middle of each month in all the countries. You can always find me only in the night but never in the day.

Answer: The alphabet "N".

ঔ

I am made up of the head of a lamb, middle of a pig, hind of a buffalo and the tail of a dragon. Who am I?

Answer: LION

ঔ

I am deaf, dumb and blind. But I am very shiny and always speak the truth. Who am I?

Answer: Mirror.

ঔ

The peacock is a bird which doesn't lay eggs. Then how does it come into the world?

Answer: Peahens lay eggs, not peacocks.

ঔ

I am transparent. You can see and feel me, but you cannot hold me. I always take the shape of my container. Who am I?

Answer: Water.

Adam is 13 years old in 1980. In 1985 he is 8 years old. How?

Answer: The dates are in BC (Before Christ).

I am a six letter word. Subtract one letter and twelve will remain. Who am I?

Answer: DOZENS.

I am a part of your body. You can hold me in your left hand but not in your right hand. Who am I?

Answer: Right hand.

I go around the world, but always stay in a corner.

Answer: Postal Stamp

When I am open I am U-shaped but when I am closed I am V-shaped. Who am I?

Answer: Umbrella.

The diametre of a hole is 4 ft 5 in. How much dirt does it contain?

Answer: A hole has no dirt in it. It contains only air.

I am so fragile that even if anybody says my name I break. Who am I?

Answer: Silence.

6 15 18 20 ? = FORTY

Answer: 25.

Explanation:

Replace each number with the corresponding letters in the alphabet.

6	=	F
15	=	O
18	=	R
20	=	T
25	=	Y

ઉ§ઈ

We are 3 friends. Our product and our sum always give the same answer. Who are we?

Answer: 1, 2, 3.

ઉ§ઈ

What occurs once in a minute, twice in a moment, but never in a thousand years?

Answer: The letter "M".

ઉ§ઈ

A grandfather, a father and 2 sons were having tea in the garden. But there are only 3 cups on the table. Justify how.

Answer: Grandfather is the father of one son and he himself also has one son. That makes two fathers and two sons.

ઉ§ઈ

Which room has no doors or windows?

Answer: A Mushroom.

ઉ§ઈ

How many times is the alphabet "a" used while writing the spelling of each number from 1 to 500?

Answer: Not a single time.

ઉ§ઈ

I have a mouth but I can't speak, I can run but I can't walk. Who am I?

Answer: A River.

ઉ§ઈ

Fill in the blank:

If Tarun's father is Bipul then Bipul is the ________ of Tarun's father.

Answer: Name.

ɞ

I have keys but can't open any lock, I have space but no room. Who am I?

Answer: Keyboard.

ɞ

You can catch me but cannot throw me. Who am I?

Answer: A cold.

ɞ

Make the following equation correct by using only 1 line:

$$102 + 5 + 8 = 650$$

Answer: 102+548=650 (use the single line to make the + 4).

ɞ

Which time of a day when written in capital letters reads the same from all the four sides?

Answer: NOON.

ɞ

Show that half of 5 equals to 4.

Answer: Remove F and E from FIVE.

IV = 4 (Roman)

ɞ

A calendar year has how many seconds?

Answer: 12 (2nd January, 2nd February, 2nd March.....)

ɞ

What gets wetter as it dries?

Answer: A towel.

What is the value of the underlined digit?

36260

Answer: Sixty.

When I get multiplied by any number the sum of the figures in the product is always me. Who I am?

Answer: 9

e.g. $9 \times 6 = 54; 5 + 4 = 9$

Find out the difference between 18°C and 64.4°F.

Answer: Zero degree.

A slice of cake costs $3 if it is cut into two pieces. How much will it cost if it is cut into seven pieces?

Answer: $3.

As the entire slice costs $3, it doesn't matter how many pieces it is cut into.

The anagram of this phrase is an instrument used in the orchestra. What is it?

A bliss nectar

Answer: Bass clarinet.

A crime is reported from 6 Park Avenue. The police reach the scene of the crime and find that a single life has been lost. The killer is also there on the spot and so are the evidences that are pointing to his crime, but the police cannot arrest him. Why?

Answer: The person who has lost his life, has killed himself. In other words, he has committed suicide.

What is the closest relationship my son can have has with my brother's niece's father's brother's mother?

Answer: She can be my son's grandmother.

ଔ୫ଚ

Complete the sentence using two words, which are anagrams.

The man with the _______ wanted to have _______.

Answer: The man with the beard wanted to have bread.

ଔ୫ଚ

A woman met one of her classmates after 20 long years. After exchanging pleasantries, the first woman told the other that she has 4 children, half of them female. At this, the other woman smiled and replied, even half of her children too are female. However, she has 3 children. How is this possible?

Answer: The second woman has all female children.

ଔ୫ଚ

Let us imagine that you are standing at the southern-most point of the earth. Now on the eastern side of that point is an island and on the western side of that point is a lake. Which one is closer to you – the island or the lake – and why?

Answer: Neither of the two because when you are standing at the southern-most point of the earth, all directions are north.

ଔ୫ଚ

Once upon a time there were two neighbours– one very rich and the other quite poor. Both were singers. While the rich man would sing in concerts, the poor man used to sing by the roadside. The rich man had this tendency to ridicule the poor man for his singing abilities. Once the poor man got infuriated and challenged the rich man that he knew all the songs in the world and could sing any existing song with whatever names the rich man could give. The rich man decided to take up the challenge and to make it more exciting promised the poor man that he would give all his wealth to him if he could really do so. He gave him the names of his four children - Arun, Sandeep, Mukesh and Prakash. The poor man sang and got all the wealth of the rich man. What song did he sing?

Answer: "Happy birthday to you. Happy birthday dear Arun. Happy birthday to you!"

"Happy birthday to you. Happy birthday dear Sandeep. Happy birthday to you!"

"Happy birthday to you. Happy birthday dear Mukesh. Happy birthday to you!"

"Happy birthday to you. Happy birthday dear Prakash. Happy birthday to you!"

"Happy birthday to you" – is an existing song and can be sung with any name of the world.

☙❧

I started learning to drive today. Just a few minutes back, I went down a one-way street in the wrong direction but I did not break the traffic rules. How?

Answer: Simple, I was not driving then, I was walking.

☙❧

An American woman living in Australia was refused a burial in India. Why?

Answer: Living people can't be buried, isn't it!

☙❧

A shepherd has 18 goats. All but 6 die. How many are left?

Answer: 6 of course!

☙❧

What comes twice in a week, once in a year, but never in a month or a day?

Answer: The Letter 'E'.

☙❧

How many two cent stamps are there in a dozen?

Answer: 12. There are 12 2-cent stamps in a dozen!

☙❧

If it took fifteen men ten days to build a tower, how long would it take four men to build it?

Answer: No time at all, as the tower it is already built!

ଔ

If there are 8 chocolates and you take away 5, how many do you have?

Answer: 5 of course. If you take 5, what else do you expect to have?

ଔ

Does the government of Texas permit a man to marry his widow's sister?

Answer: No question of legitimacy, because the man is already dead!

ଔ

Some months have 31 days, some have 30 days, how many months in the Gregorian calendar have 28?

Answer: All the 12 months!

ଔ

On an average, how many birthdays do men on earth have?

Answer: 1, just one! It is the day when we hit the earth. It is a different story that we celebrate our birthday every year, which actually implies Anniversary.

ଔ

How can you drop an egg on a floor 20 yards below, without cracking it?

Answer: The floor will not crack by the dropping of an egg on it!

ଔ

A rooster was injected with strong fertility inducing injections that could yield an average production of 10 score eggs over a period of 10 months. How many eggs would it deliver in a single day?

Answer: A rooster does not deliver eggs, it's the hen who does that!

☙❧

Why did the boy go to his bedroom with a pencil?

Answer: He wanted to draw the curtains.

☙❧

Where do fish store all their money?

Answer: On the river banks!

☙❧

How many pairs of animals did Moses take with him on his Ark to save the world's animals from the Great Flood?

Answer: It was not Moses, but Noah, who built an Ark to save the world's animals from the Great Flood.

☙❧

How can you lift a hippopotamus with one hand?

Answer: You won't find a hippo having one hand!

☙❧

What happens when an elephant sits on a chair?

Answer: It's time to buy a new chair!

☙❧

Some months have 31 days, some have 30 days, how many months in the Gregorian calendar have 28?

Answer: All the 12 months!

☙❧

On an average, how many birthdays do men on earth have?

Answer: 1, just one! It is the day when we hit the earth. It is a different story that we celebrate our birthday every year, which actually implies Anniversary.

☙❧

How can you drop an egg on a floor 20 yards below, without cracking it?

Answer: The floor will not crack by the dropping of an egg on it!

ꕥ

A rooster was injected with strong fertility inducing injections that could yield an average production of 10 score eggs over a period of 10 months. How many eggs would it deliver in a single day?

Answer: A rooster does not deliver eggs, it's the hen who does that!

ꕥ

Why did the boy go to his bedroom with a pencil?

Answer: He wanted to draw the curtains.

ꕥ

Where do fish store all their money?

Answer: On the river banks!

ꕥ

How many pairs of animals did Moses take with him on his Ark to save the world's animals from the Great Flood?

Answer: It was not Moses, but Noah, who built an Ark to save the world's animals from the Great Flood.

ꕥ

How can you lift a hippopotamus with one hand?

Answer: You won't find a hippo having one hand!

ꕥ

What happens when an elephant sits on a chair?

Answer: It's time to buy a new chair!

■■■

CHAPTER 6

Think Riddles

What four related words are merged together:
TOUS RGQC URRO IAAN RLGS EEET ENE

Answer: Orange, green, turquoise, scarlet.

Which three letter word can be placed between the two following words to make two new ones:

DON[...]HOLE

Answer: KEY.

Can you find three words which contain two consecutive i's.

Hint: The words begin with the letters R, S, T.

Answer: RADII, SKIING, TAXIING.

If I was in Florida and dropped a heavy ball into a bucket of water which was at a temperature of 45 degrees F and dropped another identical ball into an identical bucket of water at a temperature of 25 degrees F, which ball would hit the bottom of the bucket first?

Answer: The ball would reach the bottom of the 45 degree F bucket first because the water is frozen in the 25 degree F bucket!

ଓଃ

My BrainBashers electronic world atlas has developed another fault, I did a listing of miles from England to particular countries and here is the result:

Australia 500 miles

Peru 8,000 miles

India 4,500 miles

Scotland 9,500 miles

How far away did it list France as?

Answer: 3,000 miles: take the alphabetic position of the first letter, half and then multiply by 1000. F = 6, halved = 3, ab 1000 = 3,000.

ଓଃ

A man has recently escaped from prison and is making his way home on foot. He is walking along a straight rural country lane in bright daylight. He has walked about two miles from the prison, when he sees a police car coming toward him. Despite knowing that all squads would be out looking for him, he ran towards the car for a short while, and only when he was about ten feet away, did he turn and run into the woods to hide.

Why did he run towards the police car?

Answer: The man is on a bridge when he spots the police car.

He's more than halfway across, so the quickest way off the bridge is to run forward.

ଓଃ

What common English verb becomes its own past tense by rearranging its letters?

Answer: Eat ~ Ate

ଓଃ

In a box you have 13 white marbles and 15 black marbles. You also have 28 black marbles outside the box. Remove two marbles, randomly, from the box. If they are of different colours, put the white one back in the box. If they are the same colour, take them out and put a black marble back in the box. Continue this until only one marble remains in the box. What colour is the last marble?

Answer: The last marble will be WHITE.

Since marbles can only be taken out in pairs and you started off with an odd number of whites there is always going to be one white left over that you'll keep putting back in the box until it's left on it's own.

ଔ

Move just THREE crosses and flip this triangle upside down?

X

X X

X X X

X X X X

Answer:

X

X X

X X X

X X X X

Move the X

to underneath the bottom row

then move the X and X

up to each side of the new top line

X X X X

X X X

X X

X

ଔ

In the following line of letters,

cross out six letters so that the remaining letters,

without altering their sequence,

will spell a familiar English word.

B S A I N X L E A T N T E A R S

Answer:

B A N A N A

(Cross out the letters: S I X L E T T E R S)

B S A I N X L E A T N T E A R S

ꟹ

An old farmer died and left 17 cows to his three sons. In his will, the farmer stated that his oldest son should get 1/2, his middle son should get 1/3, and his youngest son should get 1/9 of all the cows. The sons, who did not want to end up with half cows, sat for days trying to figure out how many cows each of them should get.

One day, their neighbour came by to see how they were doing after their father's death. The three sons told him their problem. After thinking for a while, the neighbour said: "I'll be right back!" He went away, and when he came back, the three sons could divide the cows according to their father's will, and in such a way that each of them got a whole number of cows.

What was the neighbour's solution?

Answer: The neighbour borrowed an extra cow, to make the total number of cows 18.

Then the oldest son got 1/2 of 18 is 9 cows,

the middle son got 1/3 of 18 is 6 cows,

and the youngest son got 1/9 of 18 is 2 cows.

Since 9+6+2 = 17,

the cows could be divided among the three brothers in such a way that the borrowed cow was left over, and could be returned to its owner.

ꟹ

What is the next 3 letters in this riddle?

o t t f f s s _ _ _

Answer: E N T

They represent the first letter

when writing the numbers one thru ten.

ꕤ

On an average day, what mode of transportation carries more passengers than any other?

Answer: ELEVATOR.

ꕤ

I am something that nothing is, but yet I have a name.

I am sometimes tall and sometimes short.

I join your talks; I join your sport,

And I play in every game.

What am I?

Answer: A HANDSHAKE.

ꕤ

Though it appears to go away,

it always finds some place to stay,

devouring colours on the way.

Answer: DARKNESS.

ꕤ

Below are thirteen 5 lettered, everyday words, each of which has had two of its letters removed. In total these 26 letters are A – Z.

The remaining letters in each word are in the correct order. There are no words which are spelled differently based upon location (favour/favour, etc.) and there are no plurals. Can you determine the original words?

AAE

AVE

UIE

GON

POT

VIE

ACT

MET

BEP

UGE

LAN

RAE

BON

Answer: Amaze, brave, quiet, wagon, pivot, vixen, yacht, comet, bleep, judge, flank, grape, bonus.

What loses a head in the morning, but gains a head at night?

Answer: A pillow.

Which one of these sentences

is the odd one out?

David ushered cartooned kittens.

Simon wanted another nail.

Every artistic girl loves Easter.

Badgers rarely eat any more.

Will rabbits eat nettles?

Can rare animals nobble elephants?

Answer: Badgers rarely eat any more:

the initial letters of the words spell Bream, a fish.

The other sentences all spell birds.

Using the BrainTracker below, how many words can you find? Each word must contain the central "P" and no letter can be used twice, however, the letters do not have to be connected. Proper nouns are not allowed, however, plurals are. There is at least one nine letter word.

Excellent: 22 words. Good: 18 words. Average: 15 words.

U. R. G

A. P. T

A. H. O

Answer: All words: apart, aport, apt, atap, atop, AUTOGRAPH, gap, gorp, graph, group, hap, harp, hop, hup, op, opah, opt, ouph, pa, pah, par, para, pargo, part, pat, path, phat, phot, pht, phut, poh, port, pot, pour, pout, prahu, prao, prat, prau, pro, proa, prog, pruta, prutah, pug, pugh, pur, put, ragtop, rap, rapt, roup, tap, tapa, tarp, thorp, top, toph, trap, trop, tup, up, upo.

ଓ଼

What do these 3 have in common?

Superman

Moses

The Cabbage Patch Kids

Answer: They are all adopted !

ଓ଼

What types of animals can jump higher than a house?

Answer: ALL ... Houses can't jump

ଓ଼

I have one, you have one.

If you remove the first letter, a bit remains.

If you remove the second, bit still remains.

After much trying, you might be able to remove the third one also, but it remains.

It dies hard!

Answer:

Habit!

Remove h - a bit remains.

Remove a - bit remains.

Remove b - it remains.

ଓଃଃ

What phrase is this?

1. Stop and -

2. Start and +

3. Stay and /

4. Go and x

Answer: Go forth and multiply.

ଓଃଃ

Two men went deep into the Dutch Forest: one, a small, meek man; the other, a monster. They walked for days, until, out of food, they got desperate. The monster murdered the meek man, and ate him for dinner! He left no remains, whatsoever and was seen by no one. On his return to civilisation he told no one. Who was the murdering, canniballistic monster?

Answer: Me!

I told no one, therefore no one else could know about the incident. Only the murderer could tell the story!

ଓଃଃ

Take away my first letter; take away my second letter; take away all my letters, and I would still remain the same. What am I?

Answer: The Mail Man.

ଓଃଃ

What is put on a table, cut, but never eaten?

Answer: A Pack of Cards.

ଓଃଃ

Can you name three consecutive days without using the words Monday, Tuesday, Wednesday, Thursday, Friday, Saturday, or Sunday?

Answer: Yesterday, Today, and Tomorrow!

ଓଃ

The Pope has it but he does not use it.

Your father has it but your mother uses it.

Nuns do not need it.

Arnold Schwarzenneger has a big one,

Michael J. Fox's is quite small.

What is it?

Answer: A Last Name.

ଓଃ

What force and strength cannot get through,

I with a gentle touch can do.

And many in the street would stand,

were I not a friend at hand.

What am I?

Answer: A Key.

ଓଃ

What do bullet proof vests, fire escapes,

windshield wipers and laser printers

all have in common?

Answer: They were all invented by women.

ଓଃ

There is a barrel with no lid and some wine in it.

"This barrel of wine is more than half full," said Curly.

"No it's not," says Mo. "It's less than half full."

Without any measuring implements and without removing any wine from the barrel,

how can they easily determine who is correct?

Answer: Tilt the barrel until the wine barely touches the lip of the barrel. If the bottom of the barrel is visible then it is less than half full. If the barrel bottom is still completely covered by the wine, then it is more than half full.

ଓଃଃ

A well known seven letter word can be created, by starting with a single letter and adding a letter, one at a time, then mixing the letters, each time making a proper word. Using the clues below, which are not necessarily in the correct order, can you find all seven words. For example, A, AT, TAR, RATE, etc.

Expressing position within limits of space and time.

The subject of self-consciousness.

Frozen atmospheric vapour falling to earth.

To utter musical sounds with the voice.

Cause to oscillate.

Scattering on the earth.

The breaking of divine law.

Answer: I, in, sin, sing, swing, sowing, Snowing.

ଓଃଃ

An iron horse with a flaxen tail.

The faster the horse runs,

the shorter his tail becomes.

What is it?

Answer: A needle and thread.

ଓଃଃ

Who is your mother's

only sister's son's brother's

aunt's daughter's sister's father?

Answer: Your Father.

ଓଃଃ

Name an eight letter word that has

"kst" in the middle, in the beginning, and at the end?

Answer: Inkstand.

ଓଃ

A man walks into a pub and sits down at the bar,

and simply orders a water.

The bartender looks at the man, and then,

quickly pulls out a shotgun and points it at the man.

The man says "Thank you," and leaves.

Why did they behave this way?

Answer: The man had hiccups.

ଓଃ

At a local bar, three friends, Mr. Green, Mr. Red and Mr. Blue, were having a drink. One man was wearing a red suit; one a green suit; and the other a blue suit. "Have you noticed," said the man in the blue suit, "that although our suits have colours corresponding to our names, not one of us is wearing a suit that matches our own names?"

Mr. Red looked at the other two and said, "You're absolutely correct."

What colour suit is each man wearing?

Answer: Since none of the men are wearing the colour of suit that corresponds to their names, and Mr. Red was replying to the man in the blue suit, it had to be Mr. Green to whom he replied. We then know that Mr.Green is wearing a blue suit. Therefore, Mr. Red is wearing a green suit and Mr. Blue is wearing a red suit.

ଓଃ

Why should you never mention the number 288 in front of anyone?

Answer: Because it is

TWO GROSS

(144 = 1 gross)

ଓଃ

What 7 letter word becomes longer
when the third letter is removed?
Answer: Lounger.

ଓଃଃ

I hover out there in darkness unseen.
I will shred things to pieces 'till they're just smithereens.
I might serve as a gateway to places unspoken,
Yet I'm sealed off to man, forever unbroken.
I twist and distort, only darkness escapes,
I destroy all I find
Whatever I take.
Answer: A Black Hole/Wormhole
(as in ~ out there in the universe, not in your garden or a coalmine)

ଓଃଃ

Change the words
W A R M to C O L D in 5 changes
Answer:
One solution for transforming the word
WARM to COLD is
W A R M
W A R E
W A R D
W O R D
C O R D
C O L D

ଓଃଃ

Two convicts are locked in a cell. There is an unbarred window high up in the cell. No matter if they stand on the bed or one on top of the other they can't reach the window to escape. They then decide to tunnel out. However, they give up with the tunneling because it will take too long. Finally one of the convicts figures out how to escape from the cell.

What is his plan?

Answer: They piled the dirt dug out of the tunnel and climbed out the window from the top of the pile.

☙

A certain large animal lives happily and thrives here on Earth. One day, every single one of these critters is wiped out by a mysterious disease which affects only this particular animal. There are none left anywhere on earth — they are all gone.

About a year or so later, they begin to reappear on Earth again.

How can this be?

Answer: The animal is the Mule. Since all Mules are born sterile, you can only get a Mule by crossing a donkey with a horse. That is how the species is able to repopulate itself.

☙

What is represented by this BrainBat?

EEGVTABLES

EGVETABLES

GEEVTABLES

VEEGTABLES

Answer: MIXED VEGETABLES.

☙

I dig out tiny caves, and store gold and silver in them.

I also build bridges of silver and make crowns of gold.

They are the smallest you could imagine. Sooner or later

everybody needs my help, yet many people are afraid to

let me help them. - Who am I?

Answer: A DENTIST.

☙

Sitting at a square table are a smuggler, a mafia boss, a bootlegger and a contract killer.

Only two of these men, Mama and Kalia, are genuine criminals. The other two are CID officers posing as criminals.

Mama is sitting opposite the Mafia boss; the junior CID officer is sitting to the left of the smuggler and the senior CID officer is sitting opposite the bootlegger. If the senior officer is not playing the role of a smuggler what is the junior officer disguised as ?

Answer: THE BOOTLEGGER.

☙

I am never the first to speak

but I am always the last to be heard.

Who am I?

Answer: AN ECHO.

☙

Leather shoes are worn in bowling

and rubber-soled sneakers are worn in tennis.

In what sport are all metal shoes worn?

Answer: Horse Racing.

☙

(a) Re-arrange the following letters to form one English word:

P N L L E E E E S S S S

(b) Re-arrange the letters of NEW DOOR to make one word.

(c) What 8 letter word has 7 consonants and 1 vowel?

Hint: Tower

(d) What 5 letter word has 4 vowels and 1 consonant?

Hint: Chain

Answer:

(a) SLEEPLESSNESS.

(b) NEW DOOR

(c) STRENGTH

(d) QUEUE

ꕥ

A young boy comes from school. He lives in a high-rise building. Some days, he gets off the elevator at the eighth floor and walks up four flights to his family's apartment on the 12th floor.

On other days, he goes right up to the 12th floor. Why the difference?

Answer: He is too short to reach buttons 9 to 12.

Sometimes no one else is on the elevator.

ꕥ

Two fathers and two sons were seated round a table.

There were four apples on the table.

Each of them took one apple and ate it entirely

yet there was still one apple left on the table. How was this possible?

Answer: There were only three persons at the table

comprising a grandfather, his son and his grandson.

ꕥ

How close a relative would the sister-in-law of your father's only brother be?

Answer: Your Mother.

ꕥ

Arun was piloting a plane behind a car

but was never able to overtake it. Why?

Answer: He was on a merry-go-round

ꕥ

What do these words have in common:

age, blame, curb, dance, evidence, fence, gleam, harm, interest, jam, kiss, latch, motion, nest, order, part, quiz, rest, signal, trust, use, view, win, x-ray, yield, zone?

Answer: all the words can be used as both

VERBS and NOUNS.

ଔ

A woman from New York married ten different men from that city, yet she did not break any laws. None of these men died, and she never divorced. How was this possible?

Answer: The lady was a justice of the peace (or a minister).

ଔ

Of all the numbers whose literal representations in capital letters consists only of straight line segments (for example, FIVE), only one number has a value equal to the number of segments used to write it.

Which number has this property?

Answer: TWENTY-NINE.

ଔ

Standing on a hard floor,

How can you drop an uncooked, unpickled egg, a totally fresh untampered with egg, 3 feet without breaking it?

Answer: Start it four feet above the floor.

ଔ

A newspaper is supposed to have 60 pages

but pages 24 and 41 are missing.

Which other pages won't be there?

Answer: Pages 19, 20, 23, 37, 38, and 42

will also be missing.

ଔ

What belongs to you but others use it more than you do?

Answer: Your name.

■■■

Part II: Jokes

Chapter 7

Jokes

Air Plane Jokes

On reaching his plane seat, a man is surprised to see a parrot strapped in next to him. He asks the stewardess for a coffee where upon the parrot squawks "And get me a whisky you cow!" The stewardess, flustered, brings back a whisky for the parrot and forgets the coffee.

When this omission is pointed out to her the parrot drains its glass and bawls "And get me another whisky you idiot". Quite upset, the girl comes back shaking with another whisky but still no coffee.

Unaccustomed to such slackness the man tries the parrot's approach "I've asked you twice for a coffee, go and get it now or I'll kick you".

The next moment, both he and the parrot have been wrenched up and thrown out of the emergency exit by two burly stewards. Plunging downwards the parrot turns to him and says "For someone who can't fly, you complain too much!"

꧁

At the airport for a business trip, I settled down to wait for the boarding announcement at Gate 35. Then I heard the voice on the public address system saying, "We apologize for the inconvenience, but Delta Flight 570 will board from Gate 41."

So my family picked up our luggage and carried it over to Gate 41. Not ten minutes later the public address voice told us that Flight 570 would in fact be boarding from Gate 35.

So, again, we gathered our carry-on luggage and returned to the original gate. Just as we were settling down, the public address voice spoke again: "Thank you for participating in Delta's physical fitness programme.

꧁

Rules of the Airways

Takeoff's are optional. Landings are mandatory.

Flying is not dangerous; crashing is dangerous.

Speed is life, altitude is life insurance. No one has ever collided with the sky.

The only time you have too much fuel is when you're on fire.

Flying is the second greatest thrill known to man. Landing is the first!

Everyone knows a 'good' landing is one from which you can walk away. But a 'great landing is one after which you can use the airplane again.

The probability of survival is equal to the angle of arrival.

Was that a landing or were we shot down?

Learn from the mistakes of others. You won't live long enough to make all of them yourself.

Trust your captain.... but keep your seat belt securely fastened.

Be nice to your first officer, he may be your captain at your next airline.

Any attempt to stretch fuel is guaranteed to increase headwind.

A pilot is a confused soul who talks about women when he's flying, and about flying when he's with a woman.

Try to keep the number of your landings equal to the number of your takeoffs.

There are old pilots, and there are bold pilots, but there are no old, bold, pilots!

Gravity never loses! The best you can hope for is a draw!

Gravity SUCKS!!

Software Course

At a recent software engineering management course in the US, the participants were given an awkward question to answer. "If you had just boarded an airliner and discovered that your team of programmers had been responsible for the flight control software how many of you would disembark immediately?"

Among the ensuing forest of raised hands, only one man sat motionless. When asked what he would do, he replied that he would be quite content to stay onboard.

With his team's software, he said, the plane was unlikely to even taxi as far as the runway, let alone take off.

Cruise Ship Jokes

Once a cruise ship carrying people from all the nations was going on around the world tour when it got grounded. The ship became slow and finally came to a grinding halt.

Captain of the ship called an emergency meeting and told the passengers, "Friends, we are in trouble because of God's being angry with us. We need to give sacrifice and I need three people to sacrifice their life so that rest of us can be saved."

All of them moved towards the Deck where Japanese came forward and shouted "Long live Japan" and jumped into the sea.

Then an Israeli Jew stepped forward said "Hellulaja" and dived into the sea.

After that no one came forward for few seconds while people stared at each other and suddenly out of nowhere a Sardarji came forward near the railing and chanted,

"Jo bole-so-nihal, sat sri akaal"

"Wahe guruji da khalsa, wahe guruji di fateh"

"Jai maa Kali, Jai maa Durga, Jai Hanuman"

"Jai Sri Ram, Jai siva-sankar, Jai baba nanak di"

"Jai jawan jai kissan"

and finally yelled at the top of his voice "Bharat Mata ki jai"... and kicked the Pakistani standing next to him in the sea.

Leader Jokes

Raabri was worried whether or not Laloo upon his death made it to heaven, so she decided to try to contact his spirit. Sure enough, after the usual mumbo-jumbo of calling to the spirits, Laloo's voice was heard answering, "Hello Raabri, this is meeee..."

"Lalooji," she answered. I just have to know if you're happy there in the afterlife. What's it like there?"

"Ooooooh, it's much more beautiful here than I ever imagined," Laloo answered. "The sky is bluer, the air is cleaner, and the pastures are much more lush and green than I ever expected and above all there is no scam. And the only thing we do, all day long, are eat and sleep, eat and sleep, over and over."

"Thank God, you made it to heaven," his Raabri cried.

"Heaven?" he answered. "What heaven? I'm a buffalo in Punjab."

■■■

Chapter 8

Baby Jokes

Things Not to Say During Childbirth....

- Gosh, you're lucky. I sure wish men could experience the miracle of childbirth.
- Do you think the baby will come before Monday Night Football starts?
- I hope your ready. The Glamour Shot photographer will be here in fifteen minutes.
- If you think this hurts, I should tell you about the time I twisted my ankle playing basketball.
- That was the kids on the phone. Did you have anything planned for dinner?
- When you lay on your back, you look like a python that swallowed a wild boar.
- You don't need an epidural. Just relax and enjoy the moment.
- Oops! Which cord was I supposed to cut?

- Stop your swearing and just breathe.
- Remember what we learned in Lamaze class! HEE HEE HOO HOO. You're not using the right words.
- Your stomach still looks like there's another one in there.

ଓଃଃ

Into Labour

Deep in the back woods of Tennessee, a hillbilly's wife went into labour in the middle of the night, and the doctor was called out to assist in the delivery. Since there was no electricity, the doctor handed the father-to-be a lantern and said, "Here. You hold this high so I can see what I am doing." Soon, a baby boy was brought into the world.

Whoa there, said the doctor, "Don't be in such a rush to put that lantern down. I think there's another one coming." Sure enough, within minutes he had delivered a baby girl. "Hold that lantern up, don't set it down there's another one!" said the doctor.

Within a few minutes he had delivered a third baby.

"No, don't be in a hurry to put down that lantern, it seems there's yet another one coming!" cried the doctor.

The redneck scratched his head in bewilderment, and asked the doctor, "You imagine it might be the light that's attractin'em?

ଓଃଃ

Being a Parent

Being a parent changes everything. But being a parent also changes with each baby. Here are some of the ways having a second and third child is different from having your first.

Your Clothes

1st baby: You begin wearing maternity clothes as soon as your OB/GYN confirms your pregnancy.

2nd baby: You wear your regular clothes for as long as possible.

3rd baby: Your maternity clothes ARE your regular clothes.

Preparing for the Birth

1st baby: You practice your breathing religiously.

2nd baby: You don't bother practicing because you remember that last time, breathing didn't do a thing.

3rd baby: You ask for an epidural in your 8th month.

The Layette

1st baby: You pre-wash your newborn's clothes, colour-coordinate them, and fold them neatly in the baby's little bureau.

2nd baby: You check to make sure that the clothes are clean and discard only the ones with the darkest stains.

3rd baby: Boys can wear pink, can't they?

Worries

1st baby: At the first sign of distress - a whimper, a frown-you pick up the baby.

2nd baby: You pick the baby up when her wails threaten to wake your firstborn.

3rd baby: You teach your 3-year-old how to rewind the mechanical swing.

Chapter 9

Carpenter Jokes

Two blonde carpenters were working on a house. The one who was nailing down siding would reach into his nail pouch, pull out a nail and either toss it over his shoulder or nail it in.

The other, figuring this was worth looking into, asked, "Why are you throwing those nails away?"

The first explained, "If I pull a nail out of my pouch and it's pointed toward me, I throw it away 'cause it's defective. If it's pointed toward the house, then I nail it in!"

The second blonde got completely upset and yelled, "You moron! The nails pointed toward you aren't defective! They're for the other side of the house!"

ꕥ

A carpenter was giving evidence about an accident he had witnessed. The lawyer for the defendant was trying to discredit him and asked him how far away he was from the accident.

The carpenter replied, "Twenty-seven feet, six and one-half inches."

"What? How come you are so sure of that distance?" asked the lawyer. "Well, I knew sooner or later some idiot would ask me. So I measured it!" replied the carpenter.

ꕥ

A construction site boss was interviewing men for a job, when along came Murphy. The boss thought I'm not hiring that lazy Irishman, so he decided to set a test for Murphy, hoping he wouldn't be able to Answer the questions, and he'd be able to refuse him the job without getting into an argument.

The first question was, "Without using numbers, represent the number 9." So Murphy says, "Dat's easy," and proceeds to draw three tree's. The boss says, "What the hell's that?" Murphy says, "Tree 'n tree n'

"Tree 'n tree n' tree makes nine." Fair enough, says the boss.

Second question, same rules, but represent 99. Murphy stares into space for a while, then makes a smudge on each tree. "Der ya go sir," he says. The boss scratches his head and says, " How on earth do you get that to represent 99. Murphy says, " Each tree's dirty now! so it's dirty tree, n' dirty tree n' dirty tree, dats 99."

The boss is getting worried he's going to have to hire him, so he says, "Alright, question three. Same rules again, but represent the number 100." Murphy stares into space again, then he shouts, "Got it!" He makes a little mark at the base of each tree, and says, "There ya go sir, 100."

The boss looks at Murphy's attempt and thinks 'Ha! got him this time.' Go on Murphy, you must be mad if you think that represents a hundred."

Murphy leans forward and points to the marks at the tree bases, and says, "A little dog comes along and craps by each tree, so now you've got, dirty tree an' a turd, dirty tree an' a turd, an' dirty tree an' a turd, which makes one hundred, when do I start me job?

ઌ

A workman was killed at a construction site. The police began questioning a number of the other workers. Based with past brushes with the law, many of these workers were considered prime suspects. They were a motley crew:

The electrician was suspected of wiretapping once but was never charged.

The carpenter thought he was a stud. He tried to frame another man one time.

The glazier went to great panes to conceal his past. He still claims that he didn't do anything; that he was framed.

The painter had a brush with the law several years ago.

The heating, ventilation and air conditioning contractor was known to pack heat. He was arrested once but duct the charges.

The mason was suspect because he gets stoned regularly.

The cabinet maker is an accomplished counter fitter.

The autopsy led the police to arrest the carpenter, who subsequently confessed. The evidence against him was irrefutable, because it was found that the workman, when he died, was hammered.

CHAPTER 10

Comedy Jokes

An elderly widow and widower were dating for about five years. The man finally decided to ask her to marry. She immediately said "yes". The next morning when he awoke, he couldn't remember what her **Answer** was! "Was she happy? I think so, wait, no, she looked at me funny..." After about an hour of trying to remember to no avail he got on the telephone and gave her a call. Embarrassed, he admitted that he didn't remember her **Answer** to the marriage proposal. "Oh", she said, "I'm so glad you called. I remembered saying 'yes' to someone, but I couldn't remember who it was."

ଔଊ

A man hasn't been feeling well, so he goes to his doctor for a complete check-up. Afterward, the doctor comes out with the results. "I'm afraid I have some very bad news," the doctor says. "You're dying, and you don't have much time left." "Oh, that's terrible!" says the man. "How long have I got?" "Ten," the doctor says sadly. "Ten?" the man asks. "Ten what? Months? Weeks? What?!" The doctor interrupts, "Nine..."

ଔଊ

A man and his wife are driving down the road when a cop pulls them over.

The cop says to the man, "Do you know that you were speeding?"

The man replies, "No sir, I didn't know I was speeding."

The man's wife then yells, "Yes you did, you knew you were speeding I've been telling you to slow down for miles."

"SHUT UP!" the man says to his wife, "Shut the hell up, just sit back and be quite."

Then the cop says, "well, since I've got you pulled over did you know that the tag on your license plate is expired?"

"No Sir" the man replies, "I did not know that" "WHATEVER!" His wife yells, "I've been telling you to go get it up to date for 2 whole months now!"

"Shut up" the man tells to his wife again! "Sit back and shut up, mind your own business!"

Curious, the cop walks over to the woman's side of the car and asks her, "Does he always talk to you this way?"

"No" she replies, " Only when he's drinking!"

ଔଷଔ

One day a girl brings home her boyfriend and tells her father she wants to marry him. After talking to him for while, he tells his daughter she can't do it because he's her half brother. The same problem happens again four more times! The girl starts to get pissed off. She goes to her mom and says, "Mom... What have you been doing all your life? Dad's been going around laying every maiden in the town and now I can't marry any of the five guys I like because they have turned out to be my half brothers!!!"

Her mom replies, "Don't worry darling, you can marry any one of them you want, he isn't really your dad."

☙

A policeman was patrolling a local parking spot overlooking a golf course. He drove by a car and saw a couple inside with the dome light on. There was a young man in the driver's seat reading a computer magazine and a young lady in the back seat knitting. He stopped to investigate. He walked up to the driver's window and knocked. The young man looked up, cranked the window down, and said, "Yes Officer?"

"What are you doing?" the policeman asked. "What does it look like?" answered the young man. "I'm reading this magazine." Pointing towards the young lady in the back seat, the officer then asked, "And what is she doing?" The young man looked over his shoulder and replied, "What does it look like? She's knitting."

"And how old are you?" the officer then asked the young man. "I'm nineteen," he replied.

"And how old is she?" asked the officer.

The young man looked at his watch and said, "Well, in about twelve minutes she'll be sixteen."

☙

Once a Sadarji came home with his left forehead bleeding his wife asked him what happened.

He replied, "There was a nail in the window of the bus that pricked me each time the bus jerked."

His wife said, "Then why didn't you exchange your seat with some other passengers, that did not know about the nail!"

Sadarji replied, "How can I exchange my seat when there were no other passengers in the bus other than me."

cs80

Banta complained to a doctor that he wetted his bed every night. "Before it happens, do you see any dreams?" the doctor asked.

"Yes, doctor. Usually I see a dream in which a small demon comes and says, 'Let's pee'."

"OK," the doctor said. Next time you see the demon, say, "No, we've already peed."

Next time Banta came to the doctor, the latter asked, "So? Did you do as I said?"

"Yes, I did."

"Did it help?"

"No, doctor. Only, it made the matter worse."

"How?"

"As I said 'We've already peed,' the demon nodded and said, 'Then, let's shit a little."

cs80

A Man goes over to visit one of his friends.

While he is at her friend's house it starts to rain very heavily the type that is not going to stop. His friend tells him to spend the night at his house and go home the next day.

When he hears this, he rushes out the door and comes a while later totally drenched and carrying a small bag. So his friend asks "Where did you run off too!"

The Man says, "I went home to get my pyjamas!"

■■■

Chapter 11

Doctor Jokes

Patient: I'm in a hospital! Why am I in here?

Doctor: You've had an accident involving a bus.

Patient: What happened?

Doctor: Well, I've got some good news and some bad news. Which would you like to hear first?

Patient: Give me the bad news first.

Doctor: Your legs were injured so badly that we had to amputate both of them.

Patient: That's terrible! What's the good news?

Doctor: There's a guy in the next ward who made a very good offer on your slippers.

ଔ

A dentist, after completing work on a patient, came to him begging.

Dentist: Could you help me? Could you give out a few of your loudest, most painful screams?

Patient: Why? Docor, it wasn't all that bad this time.

Dentist: There are so many people in the waiting room right now, and I don't want to miss the four o'clock ball game.

ଔ

A woman goes to her doctor who verifies that she is pregnant. This is her first pregnancy. The doctor asks her if she has any questions. She replies, "Well, I'm a little worried about the pain. How much will childbirth hurt?"

The doctor answered, "Well, that varies from woman to woman and pregnancy to pregnancy and besides, it's difficult to describe pain."

"I know, but can't you give me some idea?" she asks.

"Grab your upper lip and pull it out a little..."

"Like this?"

"A little more..."

"Like this?"

"No. A little more..."

"Like this?"

"Yes. Does that hurt?"

"A little bit."

"Now stretch it over your head!"

ଔ

I was sitting in the waiting room of the hospital after my wife had gone into labour and the nurse walked out and said to the man sitting next to me, "Congratulations sir, you're the new father of twins!"

The man replied, "How about that, I work for the Doublemint Chewing Gum Company." The man then followed the woman to his wife's room.

About an hour later, the same nurse entered the waiting room and announced that Mr. Smith's wife has just had triplets. Mr. Smith stood up and said, "Well, how do you like that, I work for the 3M Company."

The gentleman that was sitting next to me then got up and started to leave. When I asked him why he was leaving, he remarked, "I think I need a breath of fresh air."

The man continued, "I work for 7-UP."

☙❧

A mother and her daughter were at the gynecologist's office. The mother asked the doctor to examine her daughter. "She has been having some strange symptoms and I'm worried about her," the mother said.

The doctor examined the daughter carefully and then announced, "Madam, I believe your daughter is pregnant."

The mother gasped, "That's nonsense! Why, my little girl has nothing whatsoever to do with men." She turned to the girl. "You don't, do you, dear?"

"No, mumy," said the girl. "Why, you know that I have never so much as kissed a man!"

The doctor looked from mother to daughter, and back again. Then, silently he stood up and walked to the window, staring out.

■■■

Chapter 12

Fairy Tale Jokes

Little Red Riding Hood is skipping down the road when she sees the Big Bad Wolf crouched down behind a log.

"My, what big eyes you have, Mr. Wolf," says Little Red Riding Hood.

The surprised wolf jumps up and runs away.

Further down the road Little Red Riding Hood sees the wolf again; this time he is crouched behind a tree stump.

"My, what big ears you have Mr. Wolf," says Little Red Riding Hood.

Again the foiled wolf jumps up and runs away.

About 2 miles down the road, Little Red Riding Hood sees the wolf again, this time crouched down behind a road sign.

"My, what big teeth you have Mr. Wolf," taunts Little Red Riding Hood.

With that the Big Bad Wolf jumps up and screams,

"Will you get lost? I'm trying to take a dump!"

~

Three Little Pigs went out to dinner one night.

The waiter comes and takes their drink order.

"I would like a Sprite," said the first little piggy.

"I would like a Coke," said the second little piggy.

"I want water, lots and lots of water," said the third little piggy.

The drinks are brought out and the waiter takes their orders for dinner.

"I want a nice big steak," said the first piggy.

"I would like the salad plate," said the second piggy.

"I want water, lots and lots of water," said the third little piggy.

The meals were brought out and a while later the waiter

approached the table and asked if the piggies would like any dessert.

"I want a banana split," said the first piggy.

"I want a root beer float," said the second piggy.

"I want water, lots and lots of water," exclaimed the third little piggy.

"Pardon me for asking," said the waiter! to the third little piggy,

"but why have you only ordered water all evening?"

The third piggy says,

"Well, somebody has to go 'Wee, wee, wee, all the way home!"

ଓଃଠ

A brunette is walking through the country, when she finds a bottle. She rubs it, and you guessed it, a genie appears.

The genie says, "You are allowed three wishes. But, I must warn you, anything you get, all the blondes in the world get twice as much."

The woman says, "Okay. Give me a nice house."

The genie replies, "You now have one nice house and all the blondes in the world have two."

Then the lady says, "Give me a gorgeous man."

The genie replies, "You now have one gorgeous man, while all the blondes have two."

The lady says, "For my last wish, Genie, see that stick over there? Beat me half to death with it."

■■■

Chapter 13

Funny Bones

What's the difference between chopped beef and pea soup?

Everyone can chop beef, but not everyone can pea soup!

ଓଃ

Why don't aliens eat clowns?

Because they taste funny.

ଓଃ

What do you call a fish with no eyes?

A fsh

ଓଃ

Two snowmen are standing in a field. One says to the other: "Funny, I smell carrots too".

What do you get when you cross an elephant and a rhino?

el-if-i-no

ଓଃ

Two peanuts walk into a bar.

One was a salted.

ଓଃ

Why did the fish get kicked out of school?

Cause he was caught with seaweed.

ଓଃଛ

The fight we had last night was my fault,

my wife asked me what was on the TV and I said dust.

ଓଃଛ

Boys are like parking spaces the good ones are take-in!!!!

ଓଃଛ

What did one ghost say to another?

Do you believe in people?

ଓଃଛ

Q: What is the difference between a Ph.D. in mathematics and a large pizza?

A: A large pizza can feed a family of four...

ଓଃଛ

Q: What is the difference between a mathematician and a philosopher?

A: The mathematician only needs paper, pencil, and a trash bin for his work – the philosopher can do without the trash bin...

ଓଃଛ

Q: What do you get if you add two apples and three apples?

A: A high school math problem!

ଓଃଛ

Q: What does the zero say to the the eight?

A: Nice belt!

ଓଃଛ

Q: How does one insult a mathematician?

A: You say: "Your brain is smaller than any >0!"

ଓଃଛ

Q: What does a mathematician present to his fiancée when he wants to propose?

A: A polynomial ring!

ଓଃ

Q: Why do you rarely find mathematicians spending time at the beach?

A: Because they have sine and cosine to get a tan and don't need the sun!

ଓଃ

Q: Why do mathematicians, after a dinner at a Chinese restaurant, always insist on taking the leftovers home?

A: Because they know the Chinese remainder theorem!

ଓଃ

Q: What do you get if you divide the circumference of a Jack-o-lantern by its diametre?

A: Pumpkin Pi!

Chapter 14

General Jokes

On October 15, 2004, shortly before his wedding to model Melania Knauss, Donald Trump was roasted at the Friar's Club's 100th anniversary bash in New York City. Regis Philbin led a panel of friends in razzing the Donald, among them comedian Susie Essman. "I know what Melania sees in you," she joked. "A billion dollars and high cholesterol!"

ఁఁ

A plumber attended to a leaking faucet at the neurosurgeon's house. After a two-minute job the plumber demanded 150 Rs.

The neurosurgeon exclaimed, 'I don't charge this amount even though I am a surgeon."

The plumber replied, "I agree, you are right. I too, didn't either, when I was a surgeon. That's why I switched to plumbing!"

ఁఁ

Meaning of... 'potentially' and 'realistically'

A young boy went up to his father and asked him, "Dad, what is the difference between 'potentially' and 'realistically'?"

The father thought for a moment, then answered, "Go ask your mother if she would sleep with Brad Pitt for a million dollars. Then ask your sister if she would sleep with Brad Pitt for a million dollars, and then, ask your brother if he'd sleep with Brad Pitt for a million dollars. Come back and tell me what you learn from that."

So the boy went to his mother and asked, "Would you sleep with Brad Pitt for a million dollars?"

The mother replied, "Of course, I would! We could really use that money to fix up the house and send you kids to a great university!"

The boy then went to his sister and asked, "Would you sleep with Brad Pitt for a million dollars?"

The girl replied, "Oh, good heavens! I LOVE Brad Pitt and I would sleep with him in a heartbeat. Are you nuts?"

The boy then went to his brother and asked, "Would you sleep with Brad Pitt for a million dollars?"

"Of course," the brother replied. "Do you know how much a million bucks would buy?"

The boy pondered the answers for a few days and then went back to his dad.

His father asked him, "Did you find out the difference between 'potentially' and 'realistically'?"

The boy replied, "Yes, 'Potentially', you and I are sitting on three million dollars, but 'realistically', we're living with two hookers and a future congressman."

❧

Murphy's Lesser Known Laws

Light travels faster than sound. This is why some people appear bright until you hear them speak.

He who laughs last, thinks slowest.

Change is inevitable, except from a vending machine.

Those who live by the sword get shot by those who don't.

Nothing is foolproof to a sufficiently talented fool.

The 50-50-90 rule: Anytime you have a 50-50 chance of getting something right, there's a 90% probability you'll get it wrong.

If you lined up all the cars in the world end to end, someone would be stupid enough to try to pass them, five or six at a time, on a hill, in the fog.

The things that come to those who wait will be the things left by those who got there first.

Give a man a fish and he will eat for a day. Teach a man to fish and he will sit in a boat all day drinking beer.

Flashlight: A case for holding dead batteries.

The shin bone is a device for finding furniture in a dark room.

A fine is a tax for doing wrong. A tax is a fine for doing well.

When you go into court, you are putting yourself in the hands of 12 people who weren't smart enough to get out of jury duty.

Cool Teenage Martian: I was at a party on Mercury last night.

His Friend: Was it any good?

Cool Teenage Martian: No! It was really boring.

His Friend: How come?

Cool Teenage Martian: There was no atmosphere.

Did you hear about the astronaut who stepped on chewing gum?

He got stuck in Orbit!

A Teenager is...

A person who can't remember to walk the dog but never forgets a phone number.

A weight watcher who goes on a diet by giving up candy bars before breakfast.

A youngster who receives his/her allowance on Monday, spends it on Tuesday, and borrows from his/her best friend on Wednesday.

Someone who can hear a song by Madonna played three blocks away but not his mother calling from the next room.

A whiz who can operate the latest computer without a lesson but can't make a bed.

A student who will spend 12 minutes studying for her history exam and 12 hours for her driver's license.

A youngster who is well informed about anything he doesn't have to study.

An enthusiast who has the energy to ride a bike for miles, but is usually too tired to dry the dishes.

A connoisseur of two kinds of fine music: Loud and Very Loud.

A young woman who loves the cat and tolerates her brother.

A person who is always late for dinner but always on time for a rock concert.

A romantic who never falls in love more than once a week.

A budding beauty who never smiles until her braces come off.

A boy who can sleep until noon on any Saturday when he suspects the lawn needs mowing.

An original thinker who is positive that her mother was never a teenager.

☙❧

Q. How do you keep a blonde at home?

A. Build a circular driveway.

☙❧

Lawyer: I have some good news and some bad news.

Client: Well, give me the bad news first.

Lawyer: The bad news is that the DNA tests showed that it was your blood they found all over the crime scene

Client: Oh no! I'm ruined! What's the good news?

Lawyer: The good news is your cholesterol is down to 130!

☙❧

A woman arrived at a party. While scanning the guests, she spotted an attractive man standing alone. She approached him, smiled and said, "Hello. My name is Carmen." "That's a beautiful name," he replied. "Is it a family name?" "No," she replied. As a matter of fact I gave it to myself. It represents the things that I enjoy the most – cars and men. Therefore I chose "Carmen". "What's your name?" she asked. He answered "B.J. Titsengolf."

ଔଓ

A lawyer, an economist, and a teacher were going to the bathroom. The lawyer gets done, washes his hands, and then proceeds to use almost the entire roll of paper towels to dry his hands. He says "I was taught to be thorough." The economist gets done, washes his hands, but uses only one paper towel. He says "I was taught to be environmentally friendly." The teacher gets done and leaves without washing his hands. He says "I was taught not to piss on my hands."

ଔଓ

Three sons left home, went out on their own and prospered. Getting back together, they discussed the gifts they were able to give their elderly mother. The first said, "I built a big house for our mother." The second said, "I sent her a Mercedes with a driver." The third smiled and said, "I've got you both beat. You remember how mom enjoyed reading the Bible? And you know she can't see very well. So I sent her a remarkable parrot that recites the entire Bible. It took elders in the church 12 years to teach him. He's one of a kind. Mama just has to name the chapter and verse, and the parrot recites it."

ଔଓ

Soon thereafter, mom sent out her letters of thanks: "Milton," she wrote one son, "The house you built is so huge. I live in only one room, but I have to clean the whole house."

"Gerald," she wrote to another, "I am too old to travel. I stay most of the time at home, so I rarely use the Mercedes. And the driver is so rude!"

"Dearest Donald," she wrote to her third son, "You have the good sense to know what your mother likes. The chicken was delicious."

ଔଓ

Okay, Okay, it all makes sense now... I never looked at it this way before: MENtal illness MENstrual cramps MENtal breakdown MENopause GUYnecologist And when we have REAL trouble, it's a... HISterectomy Ever notice how all of women's problems start with MEN?

꧁

Two old drunks in a bar. The first one says, "Ya know, when I was 30 and got a hard-on, I couldn't bend it with either of my hands. By the time I was 40, I could bend it about 10 degrees if I tried really hard. "By the time I was 50, I could bend it about 20 degrees, no problem. I'm gonna be 60 next week, and now I can almost bend it in half with just one hand" "So," says the second drunk, "what's your point?" "Well," says the first, "I'm just wondering how much stronger I'm gonna get!"

꧁

Q. What is the definition of a perfect lover?

A. A man with a nine inch tongue who can breath through his ears.

꧁

A man placed some flowers on the grave of his dearly departed mother and started back toward his car when his attention was diverted to another man kneeling at a grave. The man seemed to be praying with profound intensity and kept repeating, "Why did you have to die? Why did you have to die?" The first man approached him and said, "Sir, I don't wish to interfere with your private grief, but this demonstration of pain is more than I've ever seen before. For whom do you mourn so deeply? A child? A parent?" The mourner took a moment to collect himself, then replied, "My wife's first husband."

꧁

A policeman was patrolling a local parking spot overlooking a golf course. He drove by a car and saw a couple inside with the dome light on. There was a young man in the driver's seat reading a computer magazine and a young lady in the back seat knitting. He stopped to investigate. He walked up to the driver's window and knocked. The young man looked up, cranked the window down, and said, "Yes Officer?"

"What are you doing?" the policeman asked. "What does it look like?" answered the young man. "I'm reading this magazine." Pointing towards the young lady in the back seat, the officer then asked, "And what is she doing?" The young man looked over his shoulder and replied, "What does it look like? She's knitting."

"And how old are you?" the officer then asked the young man. "I'm nineteen," he replied. "And how old is she?" asked the officer. The young man looked at his watch and said, "Well, in about twelve minutes she'll be sixteen."

cxo

Daddy, how was I born ? Ah, very well, one day you need to find out anyway! Mom and Dad got together in a chat room on MSN. Dad set up a date via e-mail with your Mom and we met at a cyber cafe. We snuck into a secluded room, and then your mother downloaded from your dad's memory stick. As soon as dad was ready for an upload, it was discovered that neither one of us had used a firewall. Since it was too late to hit the delete button, nine months later the blessed virus appeared. And that's the story.

cxo

An elderly woman went into the doctor's office. When the doctor asked why she was there, she replied, "I'd like to have some birth control pills."

Taken aback, the doctor thought for a minute and then said, "Excuse me, Mrs. Sunita, but you're 75 years old. What possible use could you have for birth control pills?"

The woman responded, "They help me sleep better."

The doctor thought some more and continued, "How in the world do birth control pills help you to sleep?"

The woman said, "I put them in my granddaughter's orange juice and I sleep better at night."

ঙ্গ

A man was brought in to the hospital intensive care ward, put in a bed, tubes coming out everywhere. A week later, another man was admitted, in a similar condition.

Both lay there, machines pinging, tubes poking etc. a couple more weeks before one of them had the strength to raise his hand and point to himself and say, "Bengali."

The other patient signaled he had heard, raised his own hand, and said, "Punjabi."

This act tired them out so badly it was a week before the first summoned up the strength to say, "Calcutta."

Other replied in a weedy frail voice, "Ludhiana."

Once more, the strain was too much for them both and they passed out. Days passed before the first patient managed to again point to himself and say, "Asit."

Replied the other, "Santa."

A few hours later, Asit managed to point to himself again and rasp out weakly, "Cancer."

Santa responded, "Sagittarius."

ঙ্গ

The doctor and his wife were having a heated argument at

breakfast. As he stormed out of the house, the man angrily yelled to his wife, "You aren't that good in bed either!"

By midmorning, he decided he'd better make amends and phoned home. After many rings, his wife, clearly out of breath, answered the phone. "What took you so long to **Answer** and why are you panting?"

"I was in bed."

"What in the world are you doing in bed at this hour?"

"Getting a second opinion."

༄

The tired doctor was awakened by a phone call in the middle of the night. "Please, you have to come right over," pleaded the distraught young mother. "My child has swallowed a contraceptive."

The physician dressed quickly; but before he could get out the door, the phone rang again.

"You don't have to come over after all," the woman said with a sigh of relief. "My husband just found another one."

༄

A woman went to her doctor for a follow-up visit after the doctor had prescribed testosterone for her. She was a little worried about some of the side effects she was experiencing. "Doctor, the hormones you've been giving me have really helped, but I'm afraid that you're giving me too much. I've started growing hair in places that I've never grown hair before."

The doctor reassured her. "A little hair growth is a perfectly normal side effect of testosterone. Just where has this hair appeared?"

"On my balls."

༄

Two good friends are out driving on Route 66 and one guy has to take a leak. Being in the middle of nowhere they pull over by some shrubbery and the guy goes to relieve himself. Suddenly, he screams "Aaagh! a rattler bit my cock!"

"Relax!" says his friend, "I'll go find a pay phone and call a doctor." So his friend drives off and finds a pay phone, call a doctor and asks what he should do.

"Well," said the doc," you must cut crosses in the wound and suck out the poison."

"Is that the only way Doc?" asked the man.

☙

To get into heaven you had to walk up 100 stairs but on each stair god asks you a joke if you laugh you go to HELL.

So the Ghanta Singh gets to the 56th stair and bursts out laughing and gets sent to hell.

Then Banta Singh gets to the 97th stair and bursts out laughing and gets sent to hell.

Then the Santa Singh gets into heaven and bursts out laughing. Then god asks him, "Why are you laughing?"

Santa Singh replies, "I just got the first one!"

☙

Santa Singh was visiting his friend Banta, who had recently acquired two new dogs. He asked him what the dogs' names were. Banta said that one was named Rolex and one was named Timex.

Santa said, "Whoever heard of someone naming dogs like that?"

"HELLLOOOOOOO......," answered Banta. "They're watch dogs!"

■■■

Chapter 15

Kids Joke

Q. Why did the boy tiptoe past the medicine cabinet?

A. He didn't want to wake the sleeping pills!

ഗ്ദ്ദ

Q. How do you tease fruit?

A. Banananananananana!

ഗ്ദ്ദ

Q. Why did Rohit put a clock under his desk?

A. Because he wanted to work over-time!

ഗ്ദ്ദ

Q. Why did Rahul throw the clock out of the window?

A. Because he wanted to see time fly!

ഗ്ദ്ദ

Q. How does a moulded fruit-flavoured dessert **Answer** the phone?

A. Jell-o!

ഗ്ദ്ദ

Q. When do you stop at green and go at red?

A. When you're eating a watermelon!

Q. How did the farmer mend his pants?

A. With cabbage patches!

Q. Why don't they serve chocolate in prison?

A. Because it makes you break out!

Q. What do you call artificial spaghetti?

A. Mockaroni!

Q. What happens to a hamburger that misses a lot of school?

A. He has a lot of ketchup time!

Q. Why did the man at the orange juice factory lose his job?

A. He couldn't concentrate!

Q. How do you repair a broken Tomato?

A. Tomato Paste!

Q. Why did the baby strawberry cry?

A. Because his parents were in a jam!

Q. What did the hamburger name his daughter?

A. Patty!

Q. What kind of egg did the bad chicken lay?

A. A deviled egg!

Q. What kind of key opens the door on Thanksgiving?

A. A turkey!

ଓଃ

Q. What kind of cake do you get at a cafeteria?

A. A stomach-cake!

ଓଃ

Q. If Mr. and Mrs. Bigger had kids, who would be the biggest of the three?

A. The baby, because he's a little Bigger!

ଓଃ

Q. Why did the cookie go to the hospital?

A. He felt crummy!

ଓଃ

Q. When does a cart come before a horse?

A. In the dictionary!

ଓଃ

Q. Why were the teacher's eyes crossed?

A. She couldn't control her pupils!

ଓଃ

Q. Why did the scientist install a knocker on his door?

A. To win the Nobell Prize

ଓ଼ଷ୍ଟ

Q. Why don't mountains get cold in the winter?

A. They wear snow caps.

ଓ଼ଷ୍ଟ

Q. Why did the balloon burst?

A. Because it saw a lolly pop!

ଓ଼ଷ୍ଟ

Q. Why did it take the monster ten months to finish a book?

A. Because he wasn't very hungry.

ଓ଼ଷ୍ଟ

Q. How much do pirates pay for their earrings?

A. Buccaneer.

ଓ଼ଷ୍ଟ

Q. When is a car not a car?

A. When it turns into a garage.

ଓ଼ଷ୍ଟ

Q. What did the carpet say to the floor?

A. "You go ahead I'll cover you"

ଓ଼ଷ୍ଟ

Q. Why did the one-handed man cross the road?

A. He wanted to get to the second-hand shop!

ଓ଼ଷ୍ଟ

Q. What flower grows on your face?

A. Tulips.

ଓ଼ଷ୍ଟ

Q. What is a computer's favourite dance?

A. Disk-o

ଓ଼ଷ୍ଟ

Q. Why did the little boy put lipstick on his head?

A. He wanted to make up his mind!

ꕥ

Q. What kind of ship never sinks?

A. Friendship!

ꕥ

Q. What did the pencil sharpener say to the pencil?

A. Stop going in circles and get to the point!

ꕥ

Q. How do you make a hotdog stand?

A. Steal its chair!

ꕥ

Q. Did you hear about what happened at the Laundromat last night?

A. Three clothes-pins held up two shirts!

ꕥ

Q. Why did the computer squeak.

A. Because someone stepped on it's mouse

ꕥ

CHAPTER 16

Money Jokes

A man being mugged by two thugs put up a tremendous fight! Finally, the thugs subdued him and took his wallet. Upon finding only fifty rupees in the wallet, the surprised thug said "Why did you put up such a fight?" To which the man promptly replied "I was afraid that you would find the 2000 Rs. hidden in my shoe!"

☙

What do you get if you cross a sorceress with a millionaire?

A very witch person.

☙

Can I borrow that book of yours How To Become A Millionaire?

Sure. Here you are.

Thanks - but half the pages are missing.

What's the matter? Isn't half a million enough for you?

☙

Why is money called dough?

Because we all knead it.

☙

Where do bees keep their money?

In a honey box.

ଔ

Why did the mean teacher walk around with her purse open?

She'd read there was going to be some change in the weather.

ଔ

Fred collected lots of money from trick-or-treating and he went to the candy store to buy some chocolate.

"You should give that money to charity," said the sales girl.

Fred thought for a moment and said, "No, I'll buy the chocolate. You give the money to charity."

ଔ

What happened when the cat swallowed a coin?

There was money in the kitty.

ଔ

Three animals were having a drink in a cafe, when the owner asked for the money.

"I'm not paying," said the duck. "I've only got one bill and I'm not breaking it."

"I've spent my last buck," said the deer.

"Then the duck'll have to pay," said the skunk.

"Getting here cost me my last scent."

ଔ

Dad, would you like to save some money?

I certainly would, son.

Any suggestions?

Sure. Why not buy me a bike, then I won't wear my shoes out so fast.

ଔ

Have you heard about the new aftershave that drives women crazy?

No! Tell me about it. It smells of 500 Rs. bills.

ଔ

At the Cedar Rapids Chamber of Commerce meeting the treasurer reported a deficit of two hundred dollars.

One of the chamber members stood up and said,

"I vote that we donate half of it to the Red Cross and then give the other fifty dollars to the Salvation Army.

ᴥ

I hate paying my income tax.

You should be a good citizen – why don't you pay with a smile?

I'd like to but they insist on money!

ᴥ

The best way of saving money is to forget who you borrowed it from.

ᴥ

Rohit: Thank you so much for lending me that money. I shall be everlastingly in your debt.

Prakash: That's what I'm afraid of!

■■■

Chapter 17

Lawyer Jokes

Q. Why won't sharks attack lawyers?

A. Professional courtesy.

ଓଃ

Q. What's the definition of a lawyer?

A. A mouth with a life support system.

ଓଃ

Q. What's the definition of mixed emotions?

A. Watching your attorney drive over a cliff in your new car.

ଓଃ

Q. Have you heard about the lawyers' word processor?

A. No matter what font you select, everything comes out in fine print.

ଓଃ

Q. What do you call a smiling, sober, courteous person at a bar association convention?

A. The caterer.

ଓଃ

Q. How can you tell a lawyer is lying?

A. Other lawyers look interested.

☙❧

Q. What do you have when a lawyer is buried up to his neck in sand?

A. Not enough sand.

☙❧

Q. How can you tell when a lawyer is lying?

A. His lips are moving.

☙❧

Q. What's the difference between a lawyer and a terrorist?

A. You can negotiate with a terrorist.

☙❧

Q. What's the difference between a lawyer and a trampoline?

A. You take off your shoes before you jump on a trampoline.

☙❧

Q. If you drop a snake and an attorney off the Empire State Building, which one hits first?

A. Who cares?

☙❧

Q. What do honest lawyers and UFOs have in common?

A. You always hear about them, but you never see them.

☙❧

Q. What's the difference between a lawyer and a vulture?

A. Lawyers accumulate frequent flyer points.

☙❧

Q. What's the difference between an attorney and a pit bull?

A. Jewelry.

■ ■ ■

Chapter 18

Marriage Jokes

A man and his wife were having some problems at home and were giving each other the silent treatment. The next week the man realised that he would need his wife to wake him at 5.00 am for an early morning business flight to Chicago. Not wanting to be the first to break the silence, he finally wrote on a piece of paper, "Please wake me at 5.00 am."

The next morning the man woke up, only to discover it was 9.00 am, and that he had missed his flight. Furious, he was about to go and see why his wife hadn't woken him when he noticed a piece of paper by the bed ... it said... "It is 5.00 am; wake up."

☙

A little boy was attending his first wedding. After the service, his cousin asked him, "How many women can a man marry?"

"Sixteen," the boy responded.

His cousin was amazed that he had an **Answer** so quickly. "How do you know that?"

"Easy," the little boy said. "All you have to do is add it up, like the Bishop said: 4 better, 4 worse, 4 richer, 4 poorer"

☙

Jill and John got married. John thought this would be a "marriage of the 90's" — equal roles for equal partners. So, the first morning back from their honeymoon, he brought Jill breakfast in bed. Jill wasn't impressed with his culinary skills, however. She looked disdainfully at the tray, and snorted, "Poached? I wanted scrambled!" Undaunted, the next morning, John brought his true love a scrambled egg. Jill wasn't having any of it. "Do you think I don't like variety? I wanted poached this morning!"

Determined to please Jill, the next morning he thought, "third time's a charm" and brought her two eggs — one scrambled and one poached."Here, my love, enjoy!" Jill looks at the plate and says, "You scrambled the wrong egg."

☙❧

One of my daughter's wedding presents was a toaster oven. Soon after the honeymoon, she and her husband tried it out. Almost immediately, smoke billowed out of the toaster. "Get the owner's manual!" her husband shouted. "I can't find it anywhere!" she cried, searching through the box. "Oops!" came a voice from the kitchen. "Well, the toast is fine, but the owner's manual is burnt to a crisp."

☙❧

"Ever since we got married, my wife has tried to change me. She got me to stop drinking, smoking and running around until all hours of the night. She taught me how to dress well, enjoy the fine arts, gourmet cooking, classical music, even how to invest in the stock market," said the man. "Sounds like you may be bitter because she changed you so drastically," remarked his friend. "I'm not bitter. Now that I'm so improved, she just isn't good enough for me."

☙❧

A couple was getting married, and it was only three days before the wedding. The bride calls her mother with some bad news. "Mom," she says, "I just found out that my fiance's mother has bought the exact same dress as you to wear to the wedding." The bride's mother thinks for a minute.

"Don't worry," she tells her daughter. "I'll just go and buy another dress to wear to the ceremony." "But mother," says the bride, "that dress cost a fortune. What will you do with it? It's such a waste not to use it." "Who said I won't use it?" her mother asked. "I'll just wear it to the rehearsal dinner."

ꕥ

After Lalita brought home her fiance to meet her parents, her father invited the young man into his study to find out more about him. "What are your plans?" he asked Navjeet. "I'm a scholar of the Torah," Navjeet replied. "Well, that's admirable," Lalita's father replied. "But what will you do to provide a nice house for my daughter?" "I will study, and God will surely provide for us," Navjeet explained. "And how will you buy her a nice engagement ring?" "I will study hard, and God will provide for us." "And children?" asked the father.

"How will you support children?" "Don't worry, sir, God will provide," replied the fiancé. The conversation continued in much the same fashion. After Navjeet and Lalita had left, her mother asked her father what he found out. The father answered, "Well, he has no job and no plans, but the good news is that he thinks I'm God."

ꕥ

During the wedding rehearsal, the groom approached the pastor with an unusual offer: "Look, I'll give you $100 if you'll change the wedding vows. When you get to the part where I'm supposed to promise to 'love, honor and obey' and 'be faithful to her forever,' I'd appreciate it if you'd just leave that out." He passed the minister a $100 bill and walked away satisfied. On the day of the wedding, when it came time for the groom's vows, the pastor looked the young man in the eye and said: "Will you promise to prostrate yourself before her, obey her every command and wish, serve her breakfast in bed every morning of your life, and swear eternally before God and your lovely wife that you will not ever even look at another woman, as long as you both shall live?" The groom gulped and looked around, and said in a tiny voice, "Yes," then leaned toward the pastor and hissed: "I thought we had a deal." The pastor put a $100 bill into the groom's hand and whispered: "She made me a better offer."

ଓଃଷ

A couple had been married for 45 years and had raised a brood of 11 children and was blessed with 22 grandchildren. When asked the secret for staying together all that time, the wife replies, "Many years ago we made a promise to each other: the first one to pack up and leave has to take all the kids."

ଓଃଷ

On their 50th wedding anniversary and during the banquet celebrating it, Tarun was asked to give his friends a brief account of the benefits of a marriage of such long duration. "Tell us Tarun, just what is it you have learned from all those wonderful years with your wife?" Tarun responds, "Well, I've learned that marriage is the best teacher of all. It teaches you loyalty, meekness, forbearance, self-restraint, forgiveness — and a great many other qualities you wouldn't have needed if you'd stayed single."

ଓଃଷ

A young bride and groom-to-be had just selected the wedding ring. As the girl admired the plain platinum and diamond band, she suddenly looked concerned. "Tell me," she asked the elderly salesman "is there anything special I'll have to do to take care of this ring?" With a fatherly smile, the salesman said, "One of the best ways to protect a wedding ring is to dip it in dishwater three times a day."

ଓଃ

My wife and I have the secrets to making a marriage last...

Two times a week, we go to a nice restaurant, a little wine, good food and companionship. She goes Tuesdays. I go Fridays.

We also sleep in separate beds. Hers is in Florida, mine is in NY.

I take my wife everywhere, but she keeps finding her way back.

I asked my wife, "Where do you want to go for our anniversary?"

"Somewhere I haven't been in a long time!"

So I suggested, "How about the kitchen?"

We always hold hands. If I let go, she shops.

She has an electric blender, electric toaster, and electric bread maker. Then she said "There are too many gadgets, and no place to sit down!", so I bought her an electric chair.

My wife told me the car wasn't running well, there was water in the carburetor. When I asked where the car was, she told me "In the lake."

My wife is on a new diet. Coconuts and bananas. She hasn't lost weight, but BOY, can she climb a tree now!

She got a mudpack and looked great for two days. Then the mud fell off...

She ran after the garbage truck, yelling, "Am I too late for the garbage?" The driver said, "No, jump in!"

■■■

Chapter 19

Quick Jokes

Q. Did you hear about how quick the guy who lost his left arm and leg in a car crash?

A. He's all right now.

Q. Did you hear about the man who was tap dancing?

A. He broke his ankle when he fell into the sink.

Q. What lies at the bottom of the ocean and twitches?

A. A nervous wreck.

Q. What's the difference between roast beef and pea soup?

A. Anyone can roast beef.

Q. Where do you find a no legged dog?

A. Right where you left him.

Q. Where do you get virgin wool from?

A. Ugly sheep.

Q. Why do bagpipers walk when they play?

A. They're trying to get away from the noise.

Q. What does Star Trek and toilet paper have in common?

A. They both circle Uranus looking for Black Holes.

Q. How do you double the value of a Geo Metro?

A. Fill it with gas.

Q. What's the definition of mixed emotions?

A. When you see your mother-in-law backing off a cliff in your new car.

Q. Why do chicken coops have two doors?

A. Because if it had four doors it's be a chicken sedan.

You should always give 100% at work...

12% Monday; 23% Tuesday; 40% Wednesday; 20% Thursday; 5% Friday

Q. What do you call a cow with no legs?

A. Ground beef.

Q. What's the difference between an oral and a rectal thermometer?

A. The taste!

Q. Did you hear about the new "divorced" Barbie doll that they're selling in stores now?

A. It comes with all of Ken's stuff.

Q. What does a skeleton get when he goes to a bar?

A. A beer and a mop.

Q. What do you call Maoris on Prozac?

A. Once were worriers.

Q. How many men does it take to wallpaper a room?

A. About two – if they're thinly sliced.

Q. What's the difference between a porcupine and a Porsche?

A. The porcupine has the pricks on the outside.

Q. How many ears did Davy Crockett have?

A. Three – his left ear, his right ear, and his wild front ear.

Q. Did you hear about the blind man who went bungee jumping?

A. He loved it, but it scared the hell out of his dog.

Q. Why did the leper crash his car?

A. He left his foot on the accelerator.

Q. What do you do if you come across a tiger in the jungle?

A. Wipe him off, apologize and RUN!

Q. What do you do if an elephant comes through your window?

A. Swim!

Q. Why did the koala fall out of the tree?

A. Because it was dead.

Q. Why did the Leper go back into the shower?

A. He forgot his Head and Shoulders.

Q. What do you get when a Leper takes a bath?

A. Soup.

Q. Why did the ref call a penalty during the Leper Hockey game?

A. Because there was a face off in the corner.

Q. What's a Lepers favourite sport?

A. Football.

Q. What is Osama bin Laden's idea of safe sex?

A. Marking the camels that kick.

Q. What should Kabul get for its air defense system?

A. A refund.

Q. Why did the tree fall down?

A. The koala forgot to let go.

Q. How many male chauvinist pigs does it take to change a light bulb?

A. None, let the bitch cook in the dark.

Q. What do you do if a bird shits on your car?

A. Don't ask her out again.

Q. What do you call 100 men at the bottom of the ocean?

A. A good start.

Q. What's the difference between a woman and a computer?

A. A computer only needs the information punched into it once.

Q. Why don't cannibals eat clowns?

A. Because they taste funny.

Q. What do you call a deer with no eyes?

A. No-Eye Deer. (sound like No Idea)

Q. What do you call a deer with no eyes and no legs?

A. Still no eye deer.

Q. What do you call a deer with no eyes, no legs, and no sexual organs?

A. Still no fucking eye deer.

Q: What is the height of optimism?

A: Ganguly coming out to bat applying sunscreen on his face.

Q: What did the spectator miss when he went to the toilet?

A: The entire Indian innings.

Q: How to increase the chances of Indian batsmen playing out the entire 50 overs?

A: Try giving them two innings to begin with, then try three and so on.

Q: How should Greg Chappell reshuffle the Indian batting order?

A: Move Extras up the order.

Q: What is the Indian version of a hat-trick?

A: 3 runs in 3 balls.

Q: When would Ganguly have 100 runs against his name?

A: When he is bowling.

Q: Where do Indian Batsman perform there best?

A: In Advertisements

Q. Why are women like condoms?

A. They spend 90% of their time in your wallet, and 10% on your dick.

Q. What can a lifesaver do for a woman a man can't?

A. Cum in five different flavours.

Q. Who is the poorest guy in West Virginia?

A. The Tooth Fairy.

Q. Did you hear that Fed Ex and UPS are going to merge?

A. Yeah. They're going to call it FED UP!

Q. What's the difference between a car salesman and a computer salesman?

A. The car salesman can probably drive!

Q. Did you hear about the guy who's a dyslexic-bulimic?

A. He eats, and then he sticks his finger up his ass.

Q. What do your boss and a slinky have in common?

A. They're both fun to watch tumble down the stairs.

■■■

CHAPTER 20

Stupid Jokes

Why do morons like lightning?

They think someone is taking their picture.

ଔଊ

Why did it take the moron an hour to eat breakfast?

Because the orange juice carton instructions said Concentrate !!

ଔଊ

What do you do if a moron throws a grenade at you?

Pull the pin and throw it back at him.

ଔଊ

How did the moron fall on the floor?

He tripped over the cordless phone.

ଔଊ

How did the moron try to kill a bird?

He threw it off a mountain cliff !

ଔଊ

Why did the moron climb the glass wall ?

To see what was on the other side!

ଔଊ

How do you confuse a moron?

Put him in a round room and tell him to sit in one corner!

ঙ্গ

Hear about the moron that got an AM radio?

It took him a month to realise he could play it at night.

ঙ্গ

Why did the moron going to the airport turn around and go home?

Because he saw the sign that said "Airport Left".

ঙ্গ

Two morons were walking through the woods and they came to some tracks.

The first moron said "These look like deer tracks," and the other moron said, "No, they look like moose tracks."

They argued and argued, and they were still arguing when the train hit them.

ঙ্গ

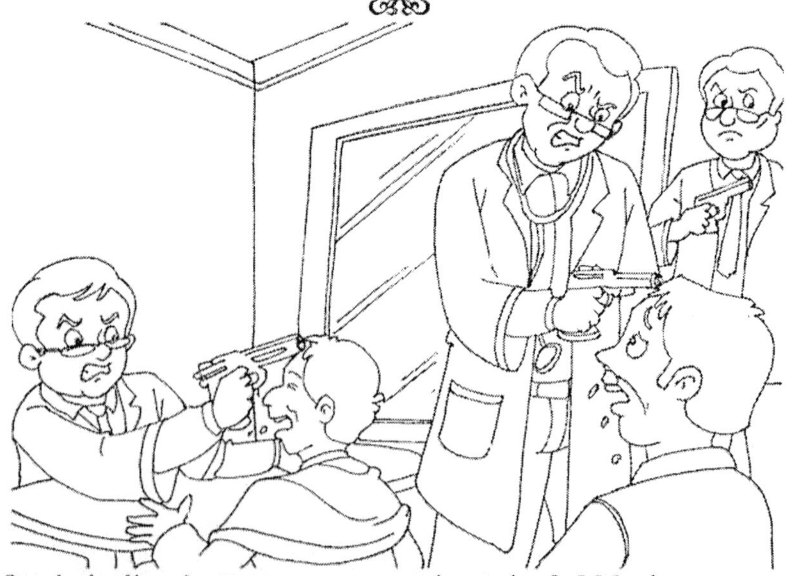

Statistically, doctors are approximately 9,000 times more dangerous than gun owners.

Remember, "Guns don't kill people, doctors do."

FACT: Not everyone has a gun, but almost everyone has at least one doctor.

Please alert your friends to this alarming threat immediately. We must ban doctors before this gets completely out of hand!

Note: Out of concern for the public at large, the statistics on lawyers have been withheld for fear the shock would cause people to panic and seek medical attention.

❧

An elderly Italian man lay dying in his bed. While suffering the agonies of impending death, he suddenly smelled the aroma of his favourite Italian anisette sprinkle cookies wafting up the stairs. Gathering his remaining strength, he lifted himself from the bed. Leaning against the wall, he slowly made his way out of the bedroom, and with even greater effort, gripping the railing with both hands, he crawled downstairs.

With laboured breath, he leaned against the door frame, gazing into the kitchen. Where if not for death's agony, he would have thought himself already in heaven, for there, spread out upon waxed paper on the kitchen table were literally hundreds of his favourite anisette sprinkled cookies.

Was it heaven? Or was it one final act of heroic love from his devoted Italian wife of sixty years, seeing to it that he left this world a happy man?

Mustering one great final effort, he threw himself towards the table, landing on his knees in a crumpled posture. His parched lips parted, the wondrous taste of the cookie was already in his mouth, seemingly bringing him back to life.

The aged and withered hand trembled on its way to a cookie at the edge of the table, when it was suddenly smacked with a spatula by his wife..... "Back off!" she said, they're for the funeral."

❧

A man walks into a doctors office one day, completely naked, and covered in saran wrap. He goes to the doctor, and the doctor does some tests, and hours later, he tells the man, "Well, I can clearly see your nuts."

ↂ

A man walks into a bar after a hellish day of work not noticing it was a gay bar. So when he walks over to order his drink, a gay meets him and said" Have you ever played bar football?" The man never heard such a thing and wanted to know how to play. The gay replied," Its very easy. All you have to do is down a pitcher of beer and fart right after. Downing the beer is a touchdown and the fart is the field goal." The man was thinking it through and thought that something might go right for a change. So the gay started the game by downing the beer and farting. He then said," Now that is seven points. Now you try." The man down the beer and when he lend over to fart, right then the gay put his finger up the man's ass and stated," Now that is how you block a field goal!"

ↂ

Once a person was eating a banana. But a guy went up to him and asked, "Where is Stanley Street? I want to know this because my name is Stanley Cup." So the person guided him to GM Place and said, "Bye!"

ↂ

Why can't a moron dial 911?

He can't find the 11 on the phone!

How do you keep a moron in suspense?

I'll tell you Tomorrow!

■■■

Chapter 21

Top Ten Jokes

Top 10 Things to do at the Mall

10. At the bottom of an escalator, scream "MY SHOELACES! AAAGH!"
9. At the stylist, ask to have the hair on your back permed.
8. Ask a saleswoman whether a particular shade of panties matches the colour of your beard.
7. Sneak up on saleswomen at the perfume counter and spray them with your own bottle of Eau de Swanke.
6. Collect stacks of paint brochures and hand them out as religious tracts.
5. At the pet store, ask if they have bulk discounts on gerbils, and whether there's much meat on them.
4. Hand a stack of pants back to the changing room attendant and scornfully announce that none of them are "leak proof".
3. Ask appliance personnel if they have any TVs that play only in Spanish.

2. Try pants on backwards at the Gap. Ask the salesperson if they make your butt look big.

1. Show people your driver's license and demand to know "whether they've seen this man."

ଔ

Top 10 Reasons Why Some Men Favour Handguns over Women?

10. You can trade in an old 44 for a new 22, no questions asked.

9. You can keep one handgun at home, and have another for when you're on the road.

8. If you admire a friend's handgun and tell him so, he will probably let you try it out a few times.

7. Your primary handgun doesn't mind if you keep another handgun for a back up.

6. Your handgun will stay with you even if you run out of ammo.

5. A handgun doesn't take up a lot of closet space.

4. Handguns function normally every day of the month.

3. A handgun doesn't ask, "do these new grips make me look fat?"

2. A handgun doesn't mind if you go to sleep after you use it.

1. You can buy a silencer for a handgun.

Chapter 22

Funny Tickers

One student fell into a cycle of classes, studying, working and sleeping.

Didn't realise how long he had neglected writing home until he received the following note:

"Dear Son, Your mother and I enjoyed your last letter. Of course, we were much younger then, and more impressionable. Love, Dad."

You automatically double-knot everything you tie.

You find yourself humming the Barney song as you do the dishes.

You hear a baby cry in the grocery store, and you start to gently sway back and forth, back and forth. However, your children are at school!

You actually start to like the smell of strained carrots mixed with applesauce.

You weep through the scene in Dumbo when his mom is taken away, not to mention what Bambi does to you.

You get soooo into crafts you contemplate writing a book called 101 Fun Crafts to do with Dryer Lint and Eggshells.

You spend a half hour searching for your sunglasses only to have your teenager say, "Mom, why don't you wear the ones you pushed up on your head?"

You are out for a nice romantic meal with your husband, enjoying some real adult conversation, when suddenly you realise that you've reached over and started to cut up his steak!

The Lone Ranger and Tonto walked into a bar one day and sat down to drink a beer.

After a few minutes, a big tall cowboy walked in and said,

"Who owns the big white horse outside?"

The Lone Ranger stood up, hitched his gunbelt, and said, "I do. Why?"

The cowboy looked at the Lone Ranger and said, "I just thought you would like to know that your horse is just about dead outside!"

The Lone Ranger and Tonto rushed outside and, sure enough, Silver was about dead from heat exhaustion. The Lone Ranger got him some water and soon Silver was starting to feel a little better.

The Lone Ranger turned to Tonto and said, "Tonto, I want you to run around Silver and see if you can create enough of a breeze to make him start to feel better."

Tonto said, "Sure Kemosabe", and took off running circles around Silver. Not able to do anything else but wait, the Lone Ranger returned to the bar to finish his drink.

A few minutes later, another cowboy struts into the bar and announces,

"Who owns that big white horse outside?"

The Lone Ranger stands again and claims, "I do. What is wrong with him this time?"

The cowboy says to him, "Nothing much, I just wanted you to know -

you left your Injun running..."

ଓଃ

These quotes were taken from actual Federal (US) employee performance evaluations...

"Since my last report, this employee has reached rock bottom and has started to dig."

"His men would follow him anywhere, but only out of morbid curiosity."

"I would not allow this employee to breed."

"This employee is really not so much of a has-been, but more of a definite won't be."

"Works well when under constant supervision and cornered like a rat in a trap."

"When she opens her mouth, it seems that it is only to change feet."

"He would be out of his depth in a parking lot puddle."

"This young lady has delusions of adequacy."

"He sets low personal standards and then consistently fails to achieve them."

"This employee is depriving a village somewhere of an idiot."

"This employee should go far, and the sooner the better."

"Got a full 6-pack, but lacks the plastic thing to hold it all together."

"A gross ignoramus – 144 times worse than an ordinary ignoramus."

"He certainly takes a long time to make his pointless."

"He doesn't have ulcers, but he's a carrier."

"I would like to go hunting with him sometime."

"He's been working with glue too much."

"He would argue with a signpost."

"He has knack for making strangers immediately."

"He brings a lot of joy whenever he leaves the room."

"When his IQ reaches 50, he should sell."

"If you see 2 people talking and one looks bored, he's the other one."

"A photographic memory but with the cap over the lens."

"A prime candidate for natural deselection."

"Donated his brain to science before he was done using it."

"Gates are down, the lights are flashing, but the train isn't coming."

"Has 2 brains, one is lost, the other is out looking for it."

"If he were any more stupid, he'd have to be watered twice a week."

"If you give him a penny for his thoughts, you'd get change."

"If you stand close enough to him, you can hear the ocean."

"It's hard to believe that he beat out 1,000 other sperm."

"One neuron short of a synapse."

"Some drink from the fountain of knowledge, he only gargled."

"Takes him 12 hours to watch 60 Minutes."

"The wheel is turning, but the hamster is dead."

ঔষ

A bird was flying south for Winter, but he had left it too late and was frozen solid in a storm.

He dropped down into a pasture of cows. The biggest, fattest cow was doing a crap there, and the bird landed in it. At first he was disgusted, until he realised the poo was thawing him out!

He started crying out for joy as the ice melted. A cat that was nearby heard the cries, walked over, saw the bird and ate it.

There are three morals to this story:

1. Not everyone who gets you into shit is your enemy.
2. Not everyone who gets you out of shit is your friend.
3. If you are in shit, keep your mouth shut.

A woman walked by and asked what they were doing. "We're supposed to find the height of the flagpole," said Bubba, "but we don't have a ladder."

The woman took a wrench from her purse, loosened a few bolts, and laid the pole down. Then she took a tape measure from her pocket, took a measurement and announced, "Eighteen feet, six inches," and walked away.

Junior shook his head and laughed. "Ain't that just like a dumb blonde! We ask for the height, and she gives us the length!"

A French guest who was staying in a hotel in Edmonton phoned room service for some pepper.

"Black pepper, or white pepper?" asked the concierge.

"Toilette pepper!"

Sardarji proposes to a woman. She says yes if you bring me a pair of crocodile boots. He sets off to Africa and disappears. Finally a search is being made. They find him hunting crocodiles and watch him killing a huge one. He walks over the reptile, checks its legs and angrily exclaims "71st and *again* barefeet!"

Khan is trying to commit suicide on the railway tracks and he takes along some wine and chicken with him.

Somebody stops him and asks "Kyon bhai, ye sab kyon leke baithe ho?" (Why do you take these things with you?).

Khan replies, "agar train late aati hai to kahin bhook se na marjaun" (If the stupid train comes late, I will die of hunger!)

☙

We all must have heard of ABCD = American Born Confused Desi...

But How about an ABCDEFGHIJKLMNOPQRSTUVWXYZ

American Born Confused Desi, Emigrated From Gujarat, Housed In Jersey, Keeping Lotsa Motels, Named Omkarnath Patel, Quickly Reached Success Through Underhanded Vicious Ways, Xenophobic Yet Zestful

☙

Indians to be sent on Moon

Manmohan Singh to Bush – We are sending Indians to the moon next year.

Bush – Wow! How Many?

Manmohan Singh - 100

25 - OBC

25 - SC

20 - ST

5 - Handicapped

5 - Sports Persons

5 - Terrorist Affected

5 - Kashmiri Migrants

9 - Politicians

and if possible 1 – Astronaut

■■■

Chapter 23

Computer Jokes

Spell Checker

I halve a spelling checker,
It came with my pea see.
It plainly marks four my revue
Mistakes I dew knot sea.
Eye strike a key and type a word
And weight four it two say
Weather eye am wrong oar write
It shows me strait aweigh.
As soon as a mist ache is maid
It nose bee fore two long
And eye can put the era rite
Its rarely ever wrong.
I've scent this massage threw it,
And I'm shore your pleased too no
Its letter prefect in every weigh;
My checker tolled me sew.

A man goes to his physician and is shocked to find that he has been replaced by a super-computer. The computer asks him his ailments and the man says he has a sore elbow. A drawer pops out and he is asked to urinate in it. After a few bleeps and flashing lights the computer decides he has tennis elbow.

The man is annoyed and decides to get one over on this machine so he asks his wife for a urine sample. He then mixes this with urine from his dog and his small son and to top it off, adds some of his sperm. He takes it to the computer-physician who again asks him for a sample. He places the urine/sperm sample in the drawer and the computer makes its usual display of bleeps and flashes before telling him that his wife is pregnant, his dog has rabies, his son has chicken pox and if he doesn't stop masturbating he'll never get rid of his tennis elbow.

A truck driver, hauling a tractor-trailer load of computers, stops for a beer. As he approaches the bar, he sees a big sign on the door that says, "COMPUTER NERDS NOT ALLOWED – ENTER AT YOUR OWN RISK!" He enters and sits down.

The bartender comes over to him, sniffs, and says that he smells kind of nerdy. He then asks him what he does for a living. The truck driver explains to him that he drives a truck, and the smell is just from the computers he is hauling. The bartender serves him a beer and says, "OK, truck drivers aren't nerds."

As he is sipping his beer, a skinny guy walks in wearing a pair of glasses with tape around the middle, a pocket protector with twelve kinds of pens and pencils, and a belt that is at least a foot too long. The bartender, without saying a word, pulls out a shotgun and blows the guy away. The truck driver asks him why he did that.

The bartender replied, "Don't worry. The computer nerds are in season because they are overpopulating Silicon Valley. You don't even need a license."

So the truck driver finishes his beer, gets back in his truck, and heads for the freeway. Suddenly, he veers to avoid an accident, and the load shifts. The back door breaks open and computers spill out all over the road. He jumps out and sees a crowd already forming, snatching up all of the computers. The scavengers are comprised of engineers, accountants and programmers – computer geeks. Each of them wearing the nerdiest clothes he has ever seen.

He can't let them steal his whole load. So remembering what happened in the bar, he pulls out his gun and starts blasting away, killing several of them instantly. A highway patrol officer comes zooming up and jumps out of the car screaming at him to stop.

The truck driver said, "What's wrong? I thought computer nerds were in season."

"Well, sure," says the patrolman, "But you can't bait 'em!"

☙❧

Bill Gates' Adventures in Heaven

Ever wondered what heaven looks like?

Bill Gates died and, much to everyone's surprise, went to Heaven. When he got there, he had to wait in the reception area.

Heaven's reception area was the size of Massachusetts. There were literally millions of people milling about, living in tents with nothing to do all day. Food and water were being distributed from the backs of trucks, while staffers with clipboards slowly worked their way through the crowd. Bill lived in a tent for three weeks until, finally, one of the staffers approached him. The staffer was a young man in his late teens, face scarred with acne. He was wearing a blue T-shirt with the words TEAM PETER emblazoned on it in large yellow lettering.

"Hello," said the staffer in a bored voice that could have been the voice of any clerk in any overgrown bureaucracy. "My name is Gabriel and I'll be your induction coordinator." Bill started to ask a question, but Gabriel interrupted him. "No, I'm not the Archangel Gabriel. I'm just a guy from Philadelphia named Gabriel who died in a car wreck at the age of 17. Now give me your name, last name first, unless you were Chinese in which case it's first name first."

"Gates, Bill." Gabriel started searching though the sheaf of papers on his clipboard, looking for Bill's Record of Earthly Works. "What's going on here?" asked Bill. "Why are all these people here? Where's Saint Peter? Where are the Pearly Gates?"

Gabriel ignored the questions until he located Bill's records. Then Gabriel looked up in surprise. "It says here that you were the president of a large software company. Is that right?"

"Yes."

"Well then, do the math chip-head! When this Saint Peter business started, it was an easy gig. Only a hundred or so people died every day, and Pankaj could handle it all by himself, no problem. But now there are over five billion people on earth. Jesus, when God said to 'go forth and multiply,' he didn't say 'like rabbits!' With that large a population, ten thousand people die every hour. Over a quarter-million people a day. Do you think Pankaj can meet them all personally?" "I guess not."

"You guess right."

So Pankaj had to franchise the operation. Now, Pankaj is the CEO of Team Pankaj Enterprises, Inc. He just sits in the corporate headquarters and sets policy. Franchisees like me handle the actual inductions." Gabriel looked though his paperwork some more, and then continued. "Your paperwork seems to be in order. And with a background like yours, you'll be getting a plum job assignment."

"Job assignment?"

"Of course. Did you expect to spend the rest of eternity sitting on your ass and drinking ambrosia? Heaven is a big operation. You have to pull your weight around here!" Gabriel took out a triplicate form, had Bill sign at the bottom , and then tore out the middle copy and handed it to Bill. "Take this down to induction centre #23 and meet up with your occupational orientator. His name is Abraham." Bill started to ask a question, but Gabriel interrupted him. "No, he's not abthatab Abraham." Bill walked down a muddy trail for ten miles until he came to induction center #23. He met with Abraham after a mere six-hour wait.

"Heaven is centuries behind in building its data processing infrastructure," explained Abraham. "As you've seen, we're still doing everything on paper. It takes us a week just to process new entries."

"I had to wait abthreeab weeks," said Bill. Abraham stared at Bill angrily, and Bill realised that he'd made a mistake. Even in Heaven, it's best not to contradict a bureaucrat. "Well," Bill offered, "maybe that Bosnia thing has you guys backed up."

Abraham's look of anger faded to mere annoyance. "Your job will be to supervise Heaven's new data processing center. We're building the largest computing facility in creation. Half a million computers connected by a multi-segment fiber optic network, all running into a back-end server network with a thousand CPUs on a gigabit channel. Fully fault tolerant. Fully distributed processing. The works."

Bill could barely contain his excitement. "Wow! What a great job! This is really Heaven!"

"We're just finishing construction, and we'll be starting operations soon. Would you like to go see the center now?"

"You bet!"

Abraham and Bill caught the shuttle bus and went to Heaven's new data processing center. It was a truly huge facility, a hundred times bigger than the Astrodome. Workmen were crawling all over the place, getting the miles of fiber optic cables properly installed. But the center was dominated by the computers. Half a million computers, arranged neatly row-by-row, half a million ....

.... Macintoshes ....

.... all running Claris software! Not a PC in sight! Not a single byte of Microsoft code!

The thought of spending the rest of eternity using products that he had spent his whole life working to destroy was too much for Bill. "What about PCs???" he exclaimed. "What about Windows??? What about Excel??? What about Word???"

"You're forgetting something," said Abraham.

"What's that?" asked Bill plaintively.

"This is Heaven," explained Abraham. "We need a computer system that's heavenly to use. If you want to build a data processing center based on PCs running Windows, then ....

.... GO TO HELL!"

ଓଃ

There was a pilot flying a small single engine charter plane, with a couple of very important executives on board. He was coming into Seattle airport through thick fog with less than 10m visibility when his instruments went out. So he began circling around looking for landmark. After an hour or so, he starts running pretty low on fuel and the passengers are getting very nervous. Finally, a small opening in the fog appears and he sees a tall building with one guy working alone on the fifth floor. The pilot banks the plane around, rolls down the window and shouts to the guy "Hey, where am I? To this, the solitary office worker replies "You're in a plane." The pilot rolls up the window, executes a 275 degree turn and proceeds to execute a perfect blind landing on the runway of the airport 5 miles away. Just as the plane stops, so does the engine as the fuel has run out.

The passengers are amazed and one asks how he did it. "Simple" replies the pilot, "I asked the guy in that building a simple question. The **Answer** he gave me was 100 per cent correct, but absolutely useless, therefore that must be Microsoft's support office and from there the airport is just a while away."

ଓଃ

MICROSOFT TESTER DIES TRAGICALLY AT HANDS OF "PAL"

REDMOND, Wa - The Microsoft Redmond Campus was rocked by tragedy today as Paul Fitzgerald, Test Engineer on the Windows NT Team, was brutally murdered in an apparently psychotic tirade by one of the "personalities" of Microsoft's latest operating system shell programme, Gaurav. In the small hours of this morning, Java, the "friendly" coffee-drinking dinosaur, burst from the screen of Fitzgerald's computer, cutting a swath of destruction throughout the hapless worker's office and into the accompanying hallway.

The beast was quickly subdued by Microsoft Campus Security upon failing to produce a valid Microsoft keycard, avoiding what could otherwise have been a tragedy of much greater proportions. He is currently undergoing psychiatric evaluation at the Washington Institute for Perfectly Valid Lifeforms Who in the Heat of the Moment Do Some Absolutely Naughty Things. Says Lars Opstad, chief spiritual healer and concert pianist, "It's touch and go right now. I don't think Java yet realises the immensity of what he's done."

Eyewitnesses say that they could hear the stegosaur-like computer guide screaming "All I wanted was a GOOD espresso" in those terrible moments before dawn. Said Rover Retriever, another Gaurav personality, "This is just terrible. Java was always such a great guy. Sure, he was a little high strung, but I can't believe he would do something like this. I think we need to seriously re-examine the stress that the Gaurav Personality group is under so that another such incident doesn't occur."

A possible precipitant to the incident could be Java's recent attempt to quit smoking as a result of a clause in his contract. Lawyers are examining whether this constitutes a violation of discriminatory hiring statutes on Microsoft's part. Microsoft Legal could not be reached for comment, but an undisclosed source asserted "We couldn't have him puffing away like that. He's a dinosaur, not a dragon. It would confuse the market."

Coroner's reports say Fitzgerald died instantly of cardiac arrest, but are unclear on whether this was a result of the vicious attack or the fact that Gaurav installed successfully on NT.

Techronia Technical Support Services

"The world of technology can be dificult for some." - Press Release

We offer a range of quality services to satisfy any possible technical support requirement. time and time again, companies rely on our services to fish their workers out of daily situations and problems. Most companies only give you the "royal shaft" treatment,

Techronia gives you the answers. We probe deep into the partially working minds of our clients and delve into their shallow waters to discover what they want from us. Whether it's the fact that they are incapable of figuring out a device like the "mouse" that 6.7 million other people know how to use, or finding that ever elusive power switch for the monitor, we are here to help.

Lets look at just some of the service offerings available from Techronia at competitive industry rates...

Techronia Priority Out of Hours Wanker Service

"I remember one client calling... It was about 2am and he used our Priority Out of Hours Wanker Service... He called saying that his screen was blank, his mind was blank, and he needed to start writing a presentation due to management the next morning." recalls technician Goldbalm. "We immediately provided a solution, by asking the user to plug the computer in, "For the thing to work, just plug it in, moron!." "It's moments like this, to hear the squeals of glee from this fucking moron that make me feel like I am doing my job." says Goldbalm shaking his head in disbelief.

It doesn't just end at simple phone support for our customeRs.. Since things like, undeleteing files clients so recklessly deleted isn't always possible, we offer stupidity consultations. We open up user groups to talk about where their stupidity originated. Heredity, social status, the fact that they received a pink slip 3 weeks ago but are still working for the company, are all group discussion topics that bring subjects into the open. Although most of the clients are irreparably moronic for the rest of their lives, we can look at ways of curving the impact of their truly stupid acts from effecting the remainder of the company.

☙❧

It was about 11:30 on a Sunday morning, when I get a request to go onto a client site. When I arrive, a man flailing his arms comes up to me and states, "I'm trying to print this document!...And the printer wont work! Why can't you guys get this printing thing right?" the user said. I approached the printer, pointed to it, and said, "Do you know what that blinking red light next to 'PAPER JAM' means?", to which there was the usual pause and, "No?" Opening the printer I exclaimed, "It means there is a fucking paper jam, as in open the printer, and take the fucking paper out, cunt." Our on-site support not only resolves the immediate problem, but helps instruct the user on how to resolve the problem in future incidences, rather then resorting to their usual complete display of arrogance.

For further information on these and many other services, contact 1-800-DUM-USER

☙❧

Some Important Instructions by a Computer Service Company...

1. When you call us to have your computer moved, be sure to leave it buried under half a ton of postcards, baby pictures, stuffed animals, dried flowers, bowling trophies and children's art. We don't have a life, and we find it deeply moving to catch a fleeting glimpse of yours.

2. Don't write anything down. Ever. We can play back the error messages from here.

3. When an I.T. person says he's coming right over, go for coffee. That way you won't be there when we need your password. It's nothing for us to remember 700 screen saver passwords.

4. When you call the help desk, state what you want, not what's keeping you from getting it. We don't need to know that you can't get into your mail because your computer won't power on at all.

5. When I.T. support sends you an E-Mail with high importance, delete it at once. We're just testing.

6. When an I.T. person is eating lunch at his desk, walk right in and spill your guts right out. We exist only to serve.

7. Send urgent email all in uppercase. The mail server picks it up and flags it as a rush delivery.

8. When the photocopier doesn't work, call computer support. There's electronics in it.

9. When something's wrong with your home PC, dump it on an I.T. person's chair with no name, no phone number and no description of the problem. We love a puzzle.

10. When an I.T. person tells you that computer screens don't have cartridges in them, argue. We love a good argument.

11. When an I.T. person tells you that he'll be there shortly, reply in a scathing tone of voice: "And just how many weeks do you mean by shortly?" That motivates us.

12. When the printer won't print, re-send the job at least 20 times. Print jobs frequently get sucked into black holes.

13. When the printer still won't print after 20 tries, send the job to all 68 printers in the company. One of them is bound to work.

14. Don't learn the proper term for anything technical. We know exactly what you mean by "My thingy blew up."

15. Don't use on-line help. On-line help is for wimps.

Tickle Me Elmo

There is a factory in Northern Minnesota which makes the Tickle

Me Elmo toys. The toy laughs when you tickle it under the arms. Well, Lena is hired at The Tickle Me Elmo factory and she reports for her first day promptly at 8:00 AM.

The next day at 8:45 AM there is a knock at the Personnel Manager's door. The Foreman throws open the door and begins to rant about the new employee. He complains that she is incredibly slow and the whole line is backing up, putting the entire production line behind schedule.

The Personnel Manager decides he should see this for himself, so the 2 men march down to the factory floor. When they get there the line is so backed up that there are Tickle Me Elmo's all over the factory floor and they're really beginning to pile up. At the end of the line stands Lena surrounded by mountains of Tickle Me Elmo's.

She has a roll of plush red fabric and a huge bag of small marbles. The 2 men watch in amazement as she cuts a little piece of fabric, wraps it around two marbles and begins to carefully sew the little package between Elmo's legs.

The Personnel Manager bursts into laughter. After several minutes of hysterics he pulls himself together and approaches Lena. "I'm sorry," he says to her, barely able to keep a straight face, "but I think you misunderstood the instructions I gave you yesterday..."

"Your job is to give Elmo two test tickles."

Chapter 24

Regular Jokes

A flying saucer landed at a gas station on a lonely country road. The two space aliens inside seemed completely unconcerned about detection; in fact, the letters "UFO" were emblazoned in big, bold letters on one side of their shiny craft. As the station owner stood and gawked in silence, paralyzed with shock, his young blonde attendant nonchalantly filled up the tank and waved to the two aliens as they took off.

"Do you realise what just happened?" the station owner finally uttered.

"Yeah," said the blonde attendant. "So?"

"Didn't you see the space aliens in that vehicle?!"

"Yeah," repeated the blonde attendant. "So?"

"Didn't you see the letters 'UFO' on the side of that vehicle?!"

"Yeah," repeated the blonde attendant. "So?"

"Don't you know what 'UFO' means?!"

The blonde attendant rolled his eyes. "Good grief, boss! I've been working here for six years. Of course, I know what 'UFO' means "Unleaded Fuel Only."

How to Annoy Your Waiter?

10. Eight hour lunch, 100 Rs. tip.
9. Ask, "Excuse me, are you a really bad singer, or a really bad actor?"
8. After he describes each special, you shout, "Garbage!"
7. Whenever he walks by, cough and mutter, "Minimum wage."
6. Every few seconds, yell, "More waffles, Cuomo!"
5. Insist that before ordering, you be allowed to touch the London broil.
4. Tie tablecloth around neck and say, "You wouldn't charge Superman for dinner, would you?"
3. Every time you eat or drink, cough really hard.
2. As he walks by to the kitchen, scream, "He's gonna spit in the chowder!"
1. Three words: eat the check.

ঙ্গ

Top Ten Things You Need To Know To Be A Nurse

10. If it's wet make it dry.
9. If it's dry make it wet.
8. Always ask for on-call pay before agreeing to overtime.
7. Never tell management what you are really thinking.
6. Never finish report with, "You have an easy assignment."
5. Never say. "This looks like a easy assignment."
4. Don't expect nurses aids to do their job.
3. Don't expect doctors to believe any thing you tell them.
2. If you don't have enough time to do everything, take about 30 minutes to complain about it.
1. If it moves, rattles, shakes, falls down, or won't stay in place: tape it.

଼

There are 2 cowboys in the kitchen. Which one is the real cowboy?

The one on the range.

Do you wanna lose ten pounds of ugly fat?

Cut off your head.

A Horse goes into a bar and the bartender says

"Hey buddy, Why the Long Face?"

Q. Where do you find a one legged dog?

A. Where you left it.

Q. What's pink and fluffy?

A. Pink fluff.

Q. What's blue and fluffy?

A. Pink fluff holding it's breath.

Two muffins are in the oven.

One says to the other "Wow it's hot in here."

The other one replies "Oh no... It's a talking muffin."

ꕥ

Baskin Robbins

Two robins were lying on their backs, basking in the sun. A mama cat and her kitten were walking by.

The kitten complained, "Mama, I'm sooo hungry, what can we eat?"

To which the mama cat, spying the two robins, replied, "How about some Baskin Robbins?"

ꕥ

Know why a room full of married people looks so empty?

There's not a Single person in it...

Don't spend $2 to dry-clean a shirt. Donate it to the Salvation Army instead. They'll clean it and put it on a hanger. Next morning buy it back for 75 cents.

Q: What did the fish say when he hit the wall?

A: DAM!!

Why do eskimos wash their clothes in Tide?

Because it's too cold "out tide!"

What do you call a boom-a-rang, that doesn't come back?

Answer: A Stick !!!

Why did the stoplight turn red?

Wouldn't you if you had to change in the middle of the street??

What is the difference between a woman and a magnet?

Magnets have a positive side!

ꕥ

Santa was visiting his son who was in America for the very first time.

Santa was at a Local Food store going up and down the aisles with his son.

Santa asked, "What is this?

Santa's son, "Powdered orange juice"

Santa a bit confused, "Powdered orange juice?"

Son: "Yeah, Dad. You just add a little water, and you have fresh orange juice."

A few minutes later, in a different aisle Santa asked again, "And what is this?

Son, "Powdered milk"

Santa, "Powdered milk??"

Son: "Yeah, Dad. You just add a little water, and you have fresh milk!"

A few minutes later, in a different aisle...

Santa, "And give a look here!! Baby Powder!! What a country, what a country!"

Chapter 25

Funny SMS Jokes

News: 3 Chimps escaped from the zoo... 1 was caught watching TV... another playing football and the third one was caught reading this Text message

The longest sentence known to man: "I do."

CNN News. Bush orders 15,000 FBI trained dogs to track down Osama. FBI awaiting further orders as one of the dogs is reading this

Crime doesn't pay...Does that mean my job is a crime?

This dog, is dog, a dog, good dog, way dog, to dog, keep dog, an dog, idiot dog, busy dog, for dog, 20 dog, seconds dog! ... Now read without the word dog.

Why were males created before females?

Cos you always need a rough draft before the final copy.

∞

TECH: Hello, Friendly Internet. May I help you?

CUSTOMER: Oh, hello young man. I was wondering if you offer online banking?

TECH: We're an Internet service provider, ma'am. You can certainly use our service to connect to online banking.

CUSTOMER: What do I need to do that?

TECH: You just need the modem in your computer. That plugs into a phone Arun. Sign up for an account, and sign up for online banking with your bank.

CUSTOMER: But where does the money come out?

TECH: I'm not sure I understand?

CUSTOMER: You know...Does the money come out from that slot on the computer?

ଓଃ

A young college co-ed came running in tears to her father. "Dad, you gave me some terrible financial advice!"

"I did? What did I tell you?" said the dad.

"You told me to put my money in that big bank, and now that big bank is in trouble."

"What are you talking about? That's one of the largest banks in the state," he said. "there must be some mistake."

"I don't think so," she sniffed. "They just returned one of my cheques with a note saying, 'Insufficient Funds'."

ଓଃ

A girl proposed Santa and he denied her simply saying that in our family, we only marry our relatives.

My mom married my dad, my brother married my bhabhi, my uncle married my aunt and so on. So please excuse me!!!!!

ଓଃ

One of my husband's duties as a novice drill instructor at Fort Jackson, S.C., was to escort new recruits to the mess hall. After everyone had made it through the chow line, he sat them down and told them, "There are three rules in this mess hall: Shut up! Eat up! Get up!" Checking to see that he had everyone's attention, he asked, "What is the first rule?" Much to the amusement of the other instructors, 60 privates yelled in unison, "Shut up, Drill Sergeant!"

ଓଃ

As the family gathered for a big dinner together, the youngest son announced that he had just signed up at an army recruiter's office. There were audible gasps around the table, then some laughter, as his older brothers shared their disbelief that he could handle this new situation. "Oh, come on, quit joking," snickered one. "You didn't really do that, did you?" "You would never get through basic training," scoffed another. The new recruited, she finally spoke, she simply asked, "Do you really plan to make your own bed every morning?"

☙❧

A drill sergeant had just chewed out one of his cadets, and as he was walking away, he turned to the cadet and said, "I guess when I die you'll come and dance on my grave." The cadet replied, "Not me, Sarge...no sir! I promised myself that when I got out of the Army I'd never stand in another line!"

☙❧

As a member of the organisation that installs computer systems aboard Navy ships, I am mindful of how important the off-ship e-mail capabilities are to sailor morale, especially when some vessels are deployed for up to six months. One day while shopping at the base commissary, I noticed another crucial aspect of my job. I was behind a frazzled mother with two active children, and as I watched, she stalked over to where her young son had perched himself on the rail of the freezer case. "If you don't get off there right now," she commanded, "I'm going to e-mail your father!"

☙❧

Reaching the end of a job interview, the Human Resources Person asked a young Engineer fresh out of Texas AandM, "And what starting salary were you looking for?" The Engineer said, "In the neighbourhood of $125,000 a year, depending on the benefits package." The interviewer said, "Well, what would you say to a package of 5 weeks vacation, 14 paid holidays, full medical and dental, a company matching retirement fund for 50% of your salary, and a company car leased every 2 years — say, a red Corvette?" The Engineer sat up straight and said, "Wow! Are you kidding?" And the interviewer replied, "Yeah, but you started it."

Walking up to a department store's fabric counter, the pretty girl said, "I would like to buy this material for a new dress. How much does it cost?" "Only one kiss per yard," replied the male clerk with a smile. "That's fine," said the girl. "I'll take ten yards." With expectation and anticipation written all over his face, the clerk quickly measured out the cloth, wrapped it up, then teasingly held it out.

The girl snapped up the package, pointed to the old geezer standing beside her, and smiled, "Grandpa will pay the bill."

One day Santa's Girlfriend asks him, Darling, on our Engagement will you give me a RING?

Santa: Ya sure. Give me your Telephone No.

A Khan was speaking to his psychiatrist. "I'm on the road a lot, and my clients are complaining that they can never reach me."

Psychiatrist: "Don't you have a phone in your car?"

Khan: "That was a little too expensive, so I did the next best thing. I put a mailbox in my car."

Psychiatrist: "Uh ... How's that working?"

Khan: "Actually, I haven't gotten any letters yet."

Psychiatrist: "And why do you think that is?"

Khan: "I figure it's because when I'm driving around, my zip code keeps changing."

Chapter 26

Instrument Jokes

Violin Jokes

What's the difference between a violin and a viola?

There is no difference. The violin just looks smaller because the violinist's head is so much bigger.

ᏠᏕᎶ

What's the difference between a violin and a fiddle?

A fiddle is fun to listen to.

ᏠᏕᎶ

Why are viola jokes so short?

So violinists can understand them.

ᏠᏕᎶ

How do you tell the difference between a violinist and a dog?

The dog knows when to stop scratching.

ᏠᏕᎶ

How many second violinists does it take to change a light bulb?

None. They can't get up that high!

ᏠᏕᎶ

Why is a violinist like a SCUD missile?

Both are offensive and inaccurate.

ᏣᏕᏈ

Why don't viola players suffer from piles (hæmorrhoids)?

Because all the assholes are in the first violin section.

ᏣᏕᏈ

What's the difference between a fiddle and a violin?

No-one minds if you spill beer on a fiddle.

ᏣᏕᏈ

Why do violinists put a cloth between their chin and their instrument?

Violins don't have spit valves.

ᏣᏕᏈ

Why should you never try to drive a roof nail with a violin?

You might bend the nail.

ᏣᏕᏈ

A violinist says to his wife, "Oh, baby, I can play you just like my violin."

His wife replies, "I'd rather have you play me like a harmonica!"

ᏣᏕᏈ

Jacques Thibault, the violinist, was once handed an autograph book by a fan while in the greenroom after a concert. "There's not much room on this page," he said. "What shall I write?"

Another violinist, standing by, offered the following helpful hint: "Write your repertoire."

ᏣᏕᏈ

"Haven't I seen your face before?" a judge demanded, looking down at the defendant.

"You have, Your Honor," the man answered hopefully. "I gave your son violin lessons last winter."

"Ah, yes," recalled the judge. "Twenty years!"

Cello Jokes

How do you get a 'cellist to play fortissimo?

Write "pp, espressivo"

ઌઌ

How do you make a cello sound beautiful?

Sell it and buy a violin.

Bass Jokes

Did you hear about the bassist who was so out of tune his section noticed?

ઌઌ

How many string bass players does it take to change a light bulb?

None; the piano player can do that with his left hand.

ઌઌ

How do you make a double bass sound in tune?

Chop it up and make it into a xylophone.

ઌઌ

How many bass players does it take to change a light bulb?

1...5...1... (1...4...5...5...1)

ઌઌ

A double bass player arrived a few minutes late for the first rehearsal of the local choral society's annual performance of Handel's Messiah.

He picked up his instrument and bow, and turned his attention to the conductor. The conductor asked, "Would you like a moment to tune?"

The bass player replied with some surprise, "Why? Isn't it the same as last year?"

ઌઌ

At a rehearsal, the conductor stops and shouts to the bass section: "You are out of tune. Check it, please!"

The first bassist pulls all his strings, says, "Our tuning is correct: all the strings are equally tight." The first violist turns around and shouts, "You bloody idiot! It's not the tension. The pegs have to be parallel!"

Lute Jokes

Lute players spend half their time tuning their instrument and the other half playing out of tune.

Harp Jokes

Why are harps like elderly parents?

Both are unforgiving and hard to get into and out of cars.

How long does a harp stay in tune?

About 20 minutes, or until someone opens a door.

What's the definition of a quarter tone?

A harpist tuning unison strings.

Piano Jokes

What do you get when you drop a piano down a mine shaft?

A flat minor.

What do you get when you drop a piano on an army base?

A flat major.

Why is an 11-foot concert grand better than a studio upright?

Because it makes a much bigger kaboom when dropped over a cliff.

Why was the piano invented?

So the musician would have a place to put his beer.

Organ Jokes

Even though I'm a violist, I realise that the organ is not a string instrument. I put the organ jokes here because I thought it made sense to put them next to the piano jokes.

What does a German Hammond organist do in his life's most tender moments?

He puts his Lalita on "slow."

ઌ

The organ is the instrument of worship for in its sounding we sense the Majesty of God and in its ending we know the Grace of God.

Woodwinds

Flute/Piccolo Jokes

How do you get two piccolos to play in unison?

Shoot one.

ઌ

Two musicians are walking down the street, and one says to the other, "Who was that piccolo I saw you with last night?"

The other replies, "That was no piccolo, that was my fife."

ઌ

Double Reed Jokes

Why is a bassoon better than an oboe?

The bassoon burns longer.

ઌ

What is a burning oboe good for?

Setting a bassoon on fire.

ઌ

What is the definition of a half step?

Two oboes playing in unison.

ઌ

What is the definition of a major second?

Two baroque oboes playing in unison.

ഏൻ

How do you get an oboist to play A flat?

Take the batteries out of his electric tuner.

ഏൻ

Why did the chicken cross the road?

To get away from the bassoon recital.

ഏൻ

What's the difference between a SCUD missile and a bad oboist?

A bad oboist can kill you.

Clarinet Jokes

How many clarinetists does it take to change a light bulb?

Only one, but he'll go through a whole box of bulbs before he finds just the right one.

ഏൻ

What's the definition of "nerd?"

Someone who owns his own alto clarinet.

ഏൻ

What do you call a bass clarinetist with half a brain?

Gifted.

ഏൻ

Saxophone Jokes

What's the difference between a saxophone and a lawn mower?

Lawn mowers sound better in small ensemles.

The neighbours are upset if you borrow a lawnmower and don't return it.

The grip.

ഏൻ

What's the difference between a baritone saxophone and a chain saw?

The exhaust.

☙

The soprano, not being smart enough to use birth control, says to her saxophophonist lover, "Honey, I think you better pull out now."

He replies, "Why? Am I sharp?"

☙

Trumpet Jokes

How many trumpet players does it take to change a light bulb?

Five. One to handle the bulb and four to tell him how much better they could have done it.

☙

What's the difference between a Trumpet player and the rear end of a horse?

I don't know either.

☙

What's the difference between trumpet players and government bonds?

Government bonds eventually mature and earn money.

☙

How to trumpet players traditionally greet each other?

"Hi. I'm better than you."

How do you know when a trumpet player is at your door?

The doorbell shrieks!

☙

Why can't a gorilla play trumpet?

He's too sensitive.

☙

In an emergency a jazz trumpeter was hired to do some solos with a symphony orchestra. Everything went fine through the first movement, when she had some really hair-raising solos, but in the second movement she started going improvising madly when she wasn't supposed to play at all.

After the concert the conductor came round looking for an explanation. She said, "I looked in the score and it said `tacit'—so I took it!"

ఌ

Trombone Jokes

What's the difference between a bass trombone and a chain saw?

Vibrato, though you can minimize this difference by holding the chain saw very still.

It's easier to improvise on a chainsaw.

ఌ

How can you make a French horn sound like a trombone?

Take your hand out of the bell and lose all sense of taste.

Take your hand out of the bell and miss all of the notes!

ఌ

How do you know when a trombone player is at your door?

The doorbell drags.

ఌ

What is a gentleman?

Somebody who knows how to play the trombone, but doesn't.

ఌ

What do you call a trombonist with a beeper and a cellular telephone?

A optimist.

ఌ

What is the difference between a dead trombone player lying in the road, and a dead squirrel lying in the road?

The squirrel might have been on his way to a gig.

ఌ

How many trombonists does it take to change a light bulb?

Just one, but he'll do it too loudly.

ଓଃଃ

How do you know when there's a trombonist at your door?

His hat says "Domino's Pizza."

ଓଃଃ

How do you improve the aerodynamics of a trombonist's car?

Take the Domino's Pizza sign off the roof.

ଓଃଃ

What kind of calendar does a trombonist use for his gigs?

"Year-At-A-Glance."

ଓଃଃ

How can you tell which kid on a playground is the child of a trombonist?

He doesn't know how to use the slide, and he can't swing.

ଓଃଃ

What is the dynamic range of the bass trombone?

On or off.

ଓଃଃ

It is difficult to trust anyone whose instrument changes shape as he plays it!

French Horn Jokes

How do you get your viola section to sound like the horn section?

Have them miss every other note.

ଓଃଃ

How can you make a trombone sound like a French horn?

Stick your hand in the bell and play a lot of wrong notes.

ଓଃଃ

What is the difference between a French horn section and a '57 Chevy?

You can tune a '57 Chevy.

ශ෴

What do you get when you cross a French Horn player and a goalpost?

A goalpost that can't march.

ශ෴

How many French horn players does it take to change a light bulb?

Just one, but he'll spend two hours checking the bulb for alignment and leaks.

ශ෴

Why is the French horn a divine instrument?

Because a man blows in it, but only God knows what comes out of it.

ශ෴

How do horn players traditionally greet each other?

"Hi. I played that last year."

"Hi. I did that piece in junior high."

ශ෴

Tuba Jokes

What's the range of a tuba?

Twenty yards if you've got a good arm!

ශ෴

How many tuba players does it take to change a light bulb?

Three! One to hold the bulb and two to drink 'till the room spins.

ශ෴

What's a tuba for?

1 1/2" by 3 1/2" unless you request "full cut."

Note: in the USA, a 2 x 4 is a two-inch by four-inch piece of wood, which actually measures 1 1/2 inches by 3 1/2 inches.

ঔ

How do you fix a broken tuba?

With a tuba glue.

ঔ

These two tuba players walk past a bar...

Well, it could happen!

Percussionist Jokes

Why are orchestra intermissions limited to 20 minutes?

So you don't have to retrain the drummers.

ঔ

What do you call someone who hangs out with musicians?

A drummer.

ঔ

What did the drummer get on his IQ test?

Drool.

ঔ

How do you know when a drummer is knocking at your door?

The knock always slows down.

ঔ

How do you get a drummer to play an accelerando?

Ask him to play in 4/4 at a steady 120 bpm.

ঔ

Why do bands have bass players?

To translate for the drummer.

■■■

Chapter 27

Leaders Jokes

The following is the list of some new viruses going round in India. Better beware of them.

P.V. Narasimha Rao Virus:

First of all, this virus reduces the CPU speed to 66Hz. Before executing any instruction, it deliberates over it a number of times and finally does nothing.

V.P. Singh Virus:

This virus reserves a quota for each instruction, and executes them only according to the quota. Needless to say, the least used instructions have a higher quota than the more used instructions. This virus is also known as social justice virus.

Sukh Ram Virus:

This virus first swallows 10% of the bits in each instruction and then executes them.

Maneka Gandhi Virus:

This is a green virus. It executes only those programmes that were written by vegetarians or animals.

L.K. Advani Virus:

This virus pops up every now and then, and the only way you can continue working is by typing Jai Shri Ram 108 times.

K.P.S. Gill Virus:

Only ladies need to worry about this virus. Every now and then the users get a whack, you know where.

Phoolan Devi Virus:

This virus hijacks all high priority processes and generates page faults for them. At times, this virus may also celebrate the CPU's birthday.

Deve Gowda Virus:

The main characteristic of this virus is that it tries to schedule all the processes at the same time. This virus services the entire request for resources, and allocates them irrespective of whether they are available or not.

Jayalalitha Virus:

This actually is a family of viruses. Each member of this virus family grab as much of hard disk space as possible, while the main virus is totally unaware of it. When everything stops working, This virus blames the user for the whole chaos.

I.K. Gujral Virus:

Before executing any instruction, this virus tries to get the approval of 18 other viruses and most of the time. one of the viruses blocks the instruction. So Gujral virus most of the time does not execute anything. While it is not doing anything, as it is always, this virus connects to the Internet and keeps sending data to all major/minor countries in the World except India w/o receiving the replies.

Veerappan Virus:

This virus plays hide and seek. it captures some resources and releases them after sometime. it sometimes seems to be eradicated but suddenly reappears.

Laloo Yadav virus:

A dangerous virus, gulps all the resources as well as it corrupts the data. If you try to use scanner. During hibernation, it will rename its signature with another deadly virus of the same family. This virus takes help from other viruses to avoid scanning.

Mulayam Virus:

Whatever way, it will try to grab resources of the system. It's only task is to abort BJP processes. This virus hangs the system by sending conflicting signals to different hardware units.

Sonia Gandhi Virus:

Once a part of most deadly virus family of the world. No scanner can detect now, how much damage it can cause to the system, but people use Bofors scanner for temporary protection.

Kashi-Maya Virus:

It's also called the Dalit virus, it destabilises the co-ordination amongst different resources. It controls & steps the low priority resources from functioning. Lots of scanners available now to kill it... other viruses are thriving by splitting this virus.

Chapter 28

War Jokes

The Sikh regiment was climbing a hill in the Kargil sector during the war when suddenly from the direction of the summit the Pakistani regiment opened fire on them. The Sikh regiment took cover behind boulders and started to return the firing. The firing continued for a long time and no progress was made so the Sikh regiment's captain thought that since the names of almost all the Pakistani soldiers are like Yusuf equal Mustafa, etc. he'll call out their names and the moment they react to the call we'll shoot them.

So he started calling out-"Yusuf" four hands shot up and they were gunned down. Then the captain called out-"Iqbal" three hands shot up and they were gunned down this continued for a few more minutes till the Pakistani's got wise and stopped responding.

The Pakistani captain then thought that at this rate all his men would be killed so he adopted the strategy of the Sikh captain and thought that all Sikhs have names rhyming with Inder like Sukhwinder, Devender, Jaswinder, etc.

So the Pakistani captain started calling out "Sukhwinder" no hands shot up from the Indian side. The Pakistani captain again called out-"Sukhwinder" still no hands shot up.

The Pakistani captain called out the same name twice again when instantly came the reply that- "Oye Sukhwinder nu kaun yaad kar-riya si?" (Who is remembering Sukhwinder?).

The Pakistani commander immediately shot up his hand and said- "Main" (me) and BANG he was shot dead.

ଓଃଡ

At the time of Indo-Pak war in 1971, Pakistan Air Force had just acquired the state of the art Sabre jet from US. The jet had some outstanding technical features which were being explained by a US instructor to some trainee Pakistani pilots. The US instructor explained the aircraft's automatic take off, automatic maneuvering, automatic supersonic acceleration, automatic weapon loading and automatic firing.

Eventually, one Pakistani pilot asked, "Sir, How do we land this aircraft?"

The US instructor said, "Son, Leave that to the Indian Air Force."

CHAPTER 29

Miscellaneous Jokes

A Sardar died and went to heaven. When he got to the pearly gate Dharam Raj told him that new rules were in effect due to the advances in education on earth.

In order to gain admittance a prospective heavenly soul must answer two questions:

1. Name two days of the week that begin with "T".

2. How many seconds are in a year?

The Sardar thought for a few minutes and answered...

1. The two days of the week that begin with "T" are Today and Tomorrow.

2. There are 12 seconds in a year.

Dharam Raj said, "OK, I'll buy the Today and Tomorrow, even though it's not the answer I expected, so your answer is correct. But how did you get 12 seconds in a year?"

The Sardar replied, "Well, January 2nd, February 2nd, March 2nd, etc...."

Dharam Raj lets him in without another word.

Once a Sadarji came home with his left forehead bleeding his wife asked him what happened.

He replied, "There was a nail in the window of the bus that pricked me each time the bus jerked."

ଓଃ

His wife said, "Then why didn't you exchange your seat with some other passengers, that did not know about the nail!"

Sadarji replied, "How can I exchange my seat when there were no other passengers in the bus other than me."

ଓଃ

WHAT IT MEANS TO HAVE A North Indian GIRL as WIFE

1. At the time of marriage, a north Indian girl has more boyfriends than her age.

2. Before marriage, she looks almost like a bollywood heroine and after marriage you have to go around her twice to completely hug her.

3. By the time she professes her undying love to you, you are bankrupt because of the number of times you had to take her out to movies, theatres and restaurants. And you wait longingly for her dowry.

4. The only dishes she can think of to cook is paneer butter masala, aloo sabji, aloo gobi sabji, aloo matar, aloo paneer, that after eating all those paneer and aloos you are either in the bed with chronic cholesterol or chronic gas disorder.

5. The only growth that you see later in your career is the rise in your monthly phone bill.

6. You are blinded by her love that you think that she is a blonde. Only later do you come to know that it is because of the mehandhi that she applies to cover her grey hair.

7. When you come home from office she is very busy watching

"Kyonki saas bhi kabi bahu thi" that you either end up eating outside or cooking yourself.

8. You are a very "ESpecial" person to her.
9. She always thought that Madras is a state and covers the whole of south India until she met you.
10. When she says she is going to "work out" she means she is going to "walk out"
11. She has greater number of relatives than the number of people you have in your home town.
12. The only two sentences in English that she knows are "Thank you" and "How are you"

WHAT IT MEANS TO HAVE A South Indian GIRL as WIFE

1. Her mother looks down at you because you didn't study in IIT or Madras / Anna University.
2. Her father starts or ends every conversation with " ... I say..."
3. She shudders if you use four letter words.
4. She has long hair, neatly oiled and braided (The Dubai based Oil Well Company will negotiate with her on a 25 year contract to extract coconut oil from her hair.)
5. She uses the word 'Super' as her only superlative.
6. Her name is another name for a Goddess or a flower.
7. Her first name is longer than your first name, middle name and surname combined (unless you are from Andhra)
8. When she mixes milk/curd and rice you are never sure whether it is for the dog or for herself.
9. For weddings, she sports a mini jasmine garden on her head

and wears silk saris in the Madras heat without looking too uncomfortable while you are melting in your singlet.

10. Her favourite cricketer is Krishnamachari Srikkanth.
11. Her favourite food is dosa though she has tried North Indian snacks like Chats (pronounced like the slang for 'conversation')
12. She bores you by telling you which raaga each song you hear is based on.
13. You have to give her jewellery, though she has already got plenty of it.
14. Her Mangal Sutra weighs more than the championship belts worn by WWF wrestlers.
15. Her father thinks she is much smarter than you.

■■■